BRF in 2001

This year we have been celebrating ten years since we moved from London to Oxford. We hope that you have been able to join us for one of our services, or a quiet day or retreat, o~ ~~~~ ~f ~h~ ~~~~ ~~h~~ ~~~~~~ ~h~~ h~~~ already taken place. If not, there end of 2001!

Services of celebration and thar

We should be delighted to welc and thanksgiving on Saturda) (preacher: Bishop Michael Turn St Edmunds Cathedral (preache tickets, please use the order form overlear.

Retreats and Quiet Days

There are still numerous retreats and quiet days in both our adult and *Barnabas* ministry programmes for September to December this year. Many are designed for those who have never been on a quiet day before. For further details visit the 'Events' section on the BRF website (www.brf.org.uk) or write to the BRF office for a copy of the full programme.

Pilgrimage to the Holy Land—April 2002

'Once you have been to the Holy Land you'll never read your Bible in the same way again.' This has been the testimony of countless pilgrims who have visited Israel—and it is certainly the experience of those who have come with BRF. During the 1990s Richard Fisher led four BRF pilgrimages to Israel, two of which were jointly led with one of BRF's trustees, Bishop John Went. A fifth BRF pilgrimage will take place 15–23 April 2002 (which is also BRF's 80th anniversary year!). This will be led by Richard Fisher and Revd Graham Usher, who is a BRF trustee, vicar of an inner-city parish in Middlesbrough, and an experienced pilgrimage leader.

For further information and booking details, please send an A4 27p s.a.e., clearly marked 'Pilgrimage' in the top left hand corner, to the BRF office in Oxford. All information is also available on the BRF website.

BRF Prayer Supporters/Partner

We have already asked all of you who read BRF notes to consider supporting our ministry work through financial giving, and we have appreciated greatly the response to this appeal. However, we are only too aware of the need for support in prayer as well, and would like to ask you to consider becoming a BRF Prayer Partner.

As a staff team we believe that in order to be effective in our ministry for BRF we need to pray regularly together. We do this here in Oxford each day at 9.00am, using the daily reading from *New Daylight*. Each day we also pray for a specific group involved with BRF—authors, trustees, booksellers, readers and staff—and for any particular needs that have arisen.

Would you be willing to commit yourself to pray regularly for BRF— for the people involved, and for our ministry? As a BRF Prayer Partner we would like to keep you informed of our prayer needs. We are now producing a bi-monthly prayer letter and we also have a prayer line telephone number, so that you can phone in each week for our latest prayer requests and news. If you would like to support BRF in this way and receive our prayer letter, please send your name and address to Richard Fisher at the BRF offices and we will add you to our mailing list. If you would prefer to receive the prayer letter by e-mail, please send your e-mail address to prayerpartner@brf.org.uk.

PLEASE NOTE BRF'S NEW ADDRESS!

In December 2000, we moved offices to north Oxford. Please note our new address and contact details:
BRF, First Floor, Elsfield Hall, 15-17 Elsfield Way, OXFORD, OX2 8FG
Telephone: 01865 319700; Fax: 01865 319701;
E-mail: enquiries@brf.org.uk

(PLEASE PRINT)

Name: _____

Address: _____

_____ Postcode: _____

Tel. (day): _____ (evening): _____

Please send me tickets for the following service(s):

                                                                    Qty

☐ Saturday 22 Sept 2001, Durham Cathedral, 2.00pm   _____
☐ Saturday 27 Oct 2001, Bury St Edmunds Cathedral, 2.00pm _____

Total number of tickets: _____

Please send your completed form to: 2001 Service Ticket Dept, BRF, First Floor, Elsfield Hall, 15–17 Elsfield Way, Oxford OX2 8FG.

Ticket applications will be processed strictly on a first-come, first-served basis. We will advise you if your application arrives after all the tickets have been allocated. If you do not hear from us, you may assume that tickets have been reserved for you as requested, and these will be despatched approximately three weeks before each service takes place.

Guidelines

VOL. 17 / PART 3   September–December 2001

Edited by **Grace Emmerson and John Parr**

Writers in this issue

Grace Emmerson is a tutor in the Old Testament for the Open Theological College. She is author of *Nahum to Malachi* in BRF's *People's Bible Commentary* series and joint-editor of *Guidelines*. Formerly she lectured in the Department of Theology in Birmingham University.

Alan Garrow is tutor in New Testament for the St Albans and Oxford Ministry Course. He is also an assistant parish priest in a benefice of seven rural parishes in Oxfordshire. His publications include *Revelation* (Routledge, 1997) and *The Ministry of the Word* (BRF, 2000). He is married to Emma.

Philip Wood is a Mennonite and Mission Development Worker with the Northwestern Synod of the United Reformed Church. He formerly worked with Leeds Nightstop and the Churches National Housing Coalition. Philip has nearly twenty years' experience with young homeless people and is currently completing research in Anabaptist-Mennonite political theology at the University of Leeds.

Michael Thompson is a Methodist minister, serving as Superintendent of the Bishop Auckland Circuit in County Durham. Formerly he taught Old Testament and Hebrew at Trinity College, Legon, Ghana. He is involved in the training of Local (Lay) Preachers, and has published a book on the Old Testament and prayer, entitled *I Have Heard Your Prayer*. He has recently completed a commentary on Isaiah 40—66.

John Parr works for a mental health charity in Suffolk and as a freelance theological educator and writer. He is joint-editor of *Guidelines*.

Trevor Dennis is well known to *Guidelines* readers for his stimulating contributions. Now Canon Chancellor of Chester Cathedral, he was formerly Vice-Principal of Salisbury and Wells Theological College. His books include *Lo and Behold! The Power of Old Testament Storytelling* and *Sarah Laughed*.

Anne Stevens was ordained in 1991 after working for several years for the home Office and British Telecom. Following a curacy in Greenwich, she spent five years in Cambridge as the Chaplin of Trinity College. She is now priest-in-charge of St Michael's, Battersea, and Director of Reader Training for the Diocese of Southwark.

The Editors write...

This issue of *Guidelines* starts with Haggai, a little-known prophet whose challenge to put God first and self second still strikes home two and a half millennia later. For a world obsessed with economic growth, Haggai's message is sobering, and asks us to consider where true *shalom* (peace, prosperity) lies.

Alan Garrow, a new contributor, writes on Revelation 6—22. His notes take an innovative approach to one of the most difficult books in the Bible. The next book couldn't be more different. Ruth is a story of family life with its ups and downs, a tale of loyalty and courage, blessing after sorrow. Behind it all God is at work in his unfailing providence. Another new contributor, Philip Wood, writes on the theme of hospitality, an important strand of biblical teaching that informs the attitudes and actions surrounding this fundamental human need.

Michael Thompson guides us through Exodus 25—40, not the easiest sections to identify with in their detailed description of the tabernacle and its furnishings. His comments range from practical queries to the meaning behind the ceremonial, the presence of God and the power of prayer. This issue's readings in Mark's Gospel concentrate on one of its leading themes, faith, and show how the faith of disciples and readers alike can be shaped by the faith of Jesus.

Advent readings focus on women in the Bible, from Eve to Mary of Nazareth. Trevor Dennis brings to life the stories of women, some well known, others unnamed. Awkward questions are not bypassed: there is here 'holy disturbance'. Anne Stevens' readings for the Christmas period concentrate on the songs found at the start of Luke's Gospel, and send us back to listen to familiar Christmas music in a fresh way.

Our thanks to all who have read *Guidelines*, written to us, and supported BRF over the year.

With all good wishes

Grace Emmerson and John Parr

John Parr writes: This is Grace's last issue as joint-editor of *Guidelines*, something she has done for ten years. I have enjoyed working with her, and I hope the notes have benefited from the friendship that has grown up between us. I know this will not be the end of Grace's involvement in BRF, because she reads BRF notes, and I hope that she will continue to write for *Guidelines* in the future.

The BRF Prayer

Almighty God, you have taught us that your word is a lamp for our feet and a light for our path. Help us, and all who prayerfully read your word, to deepen our fellowship with each other through your love. And in so doing may we come to know you more fully, love you more truly, and follow more faithfully in the steps of your son Jesus Christ, who lives and reigns with you and the Holy Spirit, one God for evermore. Amen.

Suggestions for how to use Guidelines

Set aside a regular time and place, if possible, when you can read and pray undisturbed. Before you begin, take time to be still and, if you find it helpful, use the BRF prayer.

In *Guidelines*, the introductory section provides context for the passages or themes to be studied, while the units of comment can be used daily, weekly, or whatever best fits your timetable. You will need a Bible (more than one if you want to compare different translations) as Bible passages are not included. At the end of each week is a 'Guidelines' section, offering further thoughts about, or practical application of what you have been studying.

You may find it helpful to keep a journal to record your thoughts about your study, or to note items for prayer. Another way of using *Guidelines* is to meet with others to discuss the material, either regularly or occasionally.

Naomi Starkey, Managing Editor, Bible reading notes

HAGGAI

This little book with its two short chapters (only Obadiah is shorter) is easily overlooked. As one of the 'Minor Prophets', a somewhat misleading name referring to length rather than overall significance, it is generally paid scant attention. Yet its message, brief and precisely dated even to the day of the month, is refreshingly straightforward, and its challenge to deeper commitment is inescapable.

Haggai's words belong to a single year, 520BC, and are addressed to two leaders of the Jewish community, Zerubbabel the governor and Joshua the high priest. His message isn't confined to a 'religious slot'. It is relevant to the civic life of the community too. The date is significant for understanding the message.

Haggai belongs to the time when the Jews had returned to their homeland from exile in Babylon. Their release had been swift. The Persians overthrew Babylon with surprising speed in 539BC. Soon afterwards in 538, Cyrus, the Persian king, promulgated an edict allowing the Jews and deportees of other nations to return home.

It was 18 years later when Haggai faced his contemporaries with God's challenge, time enough for them to settle down, time too for problems to develop in the community, and worse still for apathy to set in. How different it all was from the high expectations of a joyful return from exile: 'the ransomed of the Lord shall return, and come to Zion with singing… they shall obtain joy and gladness, and sorrow and sighing shall flee away' (Isaiah 51:11).

Biblical quotations are taken from the New Revised Standard Version (NRSV), but the notes can be used with whatever version you have.

1 Self first; God second

Haggai 1:1–6

Right from the opening words we are in a different world from that of earlier prophets. Isaiah's message was dated by reference to Judah's own kings (Isaiah 1:1), but times have changed. Judah is now not an independent nation but a province of the Persian empire, ruled by Cyrus' successor, Darius (522–486BC), under a governor, Zerubbabel. His name suggests that he was born in Babylon (Babel), but he is of sound Judean ancestry, in fact of David's royal line, descended from Judah's penultimate king Jehoiachin (sometimes called Jeconiah: 1 Chronicles 3:17–19).

But one thing has not changed. They are still God's people. He was with them in exile; he is with them now. The community is smaller. Its needs are different. But Haggai's message, like that of those earlier prophets, still has authority. It is 'the word of the Lord', a new challenge for a new situation, a call for transformation as befits God's people, a call to put God first.

Into the general apathy and pessimism Haggai injects a note of hope. See how he calls God 'the Lord of hosts', a title emphasizing his power, for here is a God who has changed the course of history, a bold claim the prophets were not afraid to make.

'It isn't time yet', the people say, 'to rebuild the Lord's house. Our first need is for food and shelter.' Who would quarrel with that? But has their need shaded into greed, into needless luxury with 'panelled houses', an insidious concentration on self, while God's house lies in ruins? 'Your priorities are wrong', says Haggai. 'You have put God second.' Who can forget his striking word picture in verse 6: 'you that earn wages earn wages to put them into a bag with holes'?

But a question arises for us. Is Haggai, with his emphasis on the importance of the temple, at loggerheads with such as Amos and Isaiah who had warned the people against over-concentration on the temple and its ceremonial? 'I [God] hate, I despise your festivals', says Amos (5:21). 'Trample my courts no more; bringing offerings is futile', says Isaiah (1:12–13). Yet here is Haggai reprimanding the people for not paying attention to the temple!

The hard words of those earlier prophets called for heart commitment, for worship lived out in life, not empty show. But Haggai knows that commitment to God requires visible expression, a witness to priorities, the affirmation that there is more to life than the physical and material. And this is true as much for the community as for the individual. Haggai knew well, as Israel did, that God is not confined to the temple. They had worshipped him in Babylon and known his power to save. Haggai's challenge is simply this: GOD FIRST!

2 Personal stock-taking

Haggai 1:7–11

It is easy to misunderstand this passage, even to dismiss it as superficial: rebuild the temple and all wrongs will be righted. Is God's blessing a mechanical response to what is merely external activity? Haggai's message is more honourable than that and his view of God more spiritually empowering. For Haggai, as we saw in yesterday's reading, the restoration of the temple was an outward and visible sign of renewed commitment, of the determination to put God at the centre of the community's life.

The remedy has two elements. 'First', says Haggai, 'look back, think, take stock'. But he doesn't stop there. Its counterpart is, 'take action'. Regret for the past is not enough. On its own it is a destructive emotion. God is concerned with *now*. Whatever the past has been with its failures and follies, in God's hands there is a future for us and fresh hope. There are, of course, some regrets which cannot easily be remedied. Human mortality intervenes, and the way forward lies in generous action to others still alive.

Haggai's word to his contemporaries was simple: 'Go up… fetch timber… build'. And the result, a place where God would reveal his glory, his life-giving presence. Haggai's God is a patient God. He reasons with his people, wanting to bless them. But they are people with free will, and the choice is theirs. The prophet, like others before him, was not afraid to speak of God in everyday agricultural language. They had expected a successful harvest but it came to little, so much chaff that God 'puffed' (this captures the sound of the Hebrew) it away. We may not feel comfortable with Haggai's stern words (vv. 10–11). But the prophet allows for no secondary causes. The creator is in control of nature. This is a reason for confidence, not despair. Haggai's stern words are words of hope.

Is this just a 'prosperity gospel', self-interest harnessed to bolster up the worship of God? The key word here is 'glory' (v. 8), God's presence with his people, a cause for joy but demanding, too, and often uncomfortable.

In the NT the concept of God's dwelling place has changed. 'You are the temple of God', says Paul (1 Corinthians 3:16), a solemn challenge. Are we, am I, a place where he can reveal his glory and brighten the world's darkness?

3 Partners with God

Haggai 1:12–15

Chapter 1 started with apathy and self-interest. It ends with enthusiasm and joyful co-operation. And the reason? We find it in today's passage. First, response to the prophet's challenge, then action. Response meant work, hard work, not sentimental devotion but robust commitment. They feared/revered the Lord. And then came that promise of all promises, 'I am with you.' Amid the flurry of activity God's promise is brief: four words in English, two in Hebrew.

The expression, 'says the Lord', is a particularly solemn declaration here, its tone better captured by the more formal phrase, 'utterance of the Lord'. It was God's promise, not synthetic, transient enthusiasm, which motivated the activity, leaders and people working together in harmony, in response to God's initiative. The rebuilding begun that day in 520 lasted through many centuries until finally destroyed by Pompey's armies in 63BC.

Two other words are especially worth reflecting on before we leave this chapter. The first is the term 'sent' (v. 12). This is the source of Haggai's authority, his credentials to bear the Lord's message. It is the Hebrew equivalent of the Greek word from which 'apostle' comes. The other term is 'remnant', a common enough word in everyday usage for leftovers such as cloth, available cheaply. There is nothing cheap about God's 'remnant'. Its cost is unwearying love. Whatever disasters befall God's people, however much they live their lives without him, God does not give up. He treasures the seed, however small, which will germinate into hope. The word 'remnant' denotes both sadness and confidence. In the past things have gone wrong but the future lies with God.

4 God keeps his promise

Seven weeks have elapsed since Haggai's first challenge to the dispirited community. Now it is the day of the great annual festival, the Feast of Tabernacles or Booths when Israel celebrated its rescue from Egypt and its years of desert journeys. (Leviticus 23:39–43 sets out the detailed requirements.) This festival setting gives the clue to Haggai's mention of the exodus from Egypt (v. 5).

It is not for nothing that Haggai's name is given in verse 1. The prophet's identity is important. He is no mere robot devoid of personality but a man chosen by God for a special task. The rebuilt temple couldn't match the magnificence of Solomon's temple, but it was still a symbol of commitment. And symbols are powerful expressions of spiritual truths which are independent of them yet signified by them.

God doesn't skimp on encouragement, nor should his messengers! Three times Haggai repeats, 'take courage', for Zerubbabel, for Joshua and for the people. And this courage is not just wishful thinking but grounded in the promise, 'I am with you', an intensely personal relationship promised by the risen Jesus to all his followers (Matthew 28:20).

The oldest folk in Haggai's time would just be able to remember the temple before it was ravaged by the Babylonians. But God's memory is longer still. Years before even the first temple existed, he saved Israel from Egypt, a slave people rescued in defiance of the great Pharaoh's will.

Behind the imagery of verses 6 and 7, 'I will shake the heavens and the earth… and I will shake all the nations' lies either an allusion to storms which shake the ripe fruit from the trees or possibly a sidelong glance at historical upheavals in the Persian empire as rivals struggled for the throne. Whichever it is, the prophet knows that the Lord's presence does bring disturbance. Notice, too, the word 'all' by which Haggai affirms God's sovereignty. The riches of one nation alone are not sufficient for his honour.

As often in the prophets there is a foreshortening of the time scale, 'in a little while', much as in the earliest NT writings when they

11

looked for Christ's imminent return (1 Thessalonians 4:15). The final promise of this passage is *shalom* (v. 9). How best to translate it? NRSV has 'prosperity'; NIV 'peace'; REB 'prosperity and peace'. More than material prosperity is conveyed by this Hebrew word. It is well-being in the deepest sense, the renewal of relationships between people and above all between them and God.

5 Is holiness contagious?

Haggai 2:10–19

A strange, abstruse question we may feel, but for Haggai it is a practical matter! In visionary mode he has looked into the future. Now he comes down to earth, to questions of uncleanness and holiness. Which is contagious, asks Haggai, holiness or uncleanness? But let us not write it off as an abstruse point of antiquated law! Look further. It is a direct challenge to his contemporaries with practical implications about the reality of their relationship to God.

He puts his questions to the priests. One of their main functions was to interpret the law and instruct the people in its obedience. Just as health cannot be passed on but disease can, so, in Haggai's thinking, the same is true of holiness and uncleanness.

By this time the work of rebuilding the temple had continued for three months. But discouragement was setting in again. A new challenge was needed. Holiness is not contagious, nor can rebuilding the temple and observing its ceremonial make the worshippers holy. Spirituality can be expressed in ritual but never replaced by it. It demands genuine commitment. To suppose that God responds to outward observance without the transformation of the worshippers is a denial of his nature as the life-giving, life-changing God. He invites us into a *meaningful* relationship with him.

Yet uncleanness, like disease, *is* contagious. Unholy worshippers render their offerings unacceptable. But with God there is always the possibility of a fresh start—'from this day on I will bless you' (v. 19), a promise for us too.

6 The Messiah foreshadowed

The book of Haggai, which started in so down-to-earth a fashion about dissatisfaction in employment, wrong priorities in life, ends on a visionary note. Here is a reminder that the words of prophets, those mysterious messengers from God, had a relevance beyond their contemporaries. Their messages were born out of specific circumstances and addressed to particular needs, but they embraced a wider horizon hinting, in what we might call impressionistic form, at what was yet to be. Logic with its cold parameters of human reason is at odds with the prophets who spoke of a greater, yet unseen, reality.

Haggai had already spoken of the wealth of nations flowing into God's house, a reminder that all earth's wealth, and heaven's too, belong to the Lord. But here, in his last words, kingdoms, nations and all the trappings of their power are to be overthrown. Those who have lived by the sword will ultimately die by the sword.

Haggai was not a political agitator, a revolutionary. He was speaking not in literal, historical terms of disturbances within the Persian empire but of God's action on a grander scale against everything that opposes his rule. This is a scene not of human making. Repeating his earlier expression, 'I am about to shake the heavens and the earth', he indicates that this is God's doing without human participation. Amid the wreckage of earth's empires God will remain unique and sovereign.

Great hopes for the future were focused on Zerubbabel, Judah's governor, undergirded by his royal descent. The terms applied to him here are messianic. He is God's servant, chosen to bear his kingly authority, just as letters or decrees sealed with the king's signet carried royal authority, as truly as if the king himself were present.

But Zerubbabel soon disappeared from the pages of history. What befell him we do not know. The fulfilment of the promise had to await another Son of David's line, destined to be not only God's servant but his suffering one, thus fulfilling, too, the vision of that other prophet, Isaiah:

he was wounded for our transgressions,
crushed for our iniquities:
upon him was the punishment that made us whole,
and by his bruises we are healed. (Isaiah 53:5)

Guidelines

Haggai spoke of the treasures of all nations enriching God's house. In symbolic fashion the gospel story tells of wise men from the east bringing treasures to the one in whom God's presence came to dwell (John 2:19–21). Haggai's words of hope come to an abrupt end. Though glimpsing a great future his vision was restricted, time-bound in particular circumstances. His hopes were fulfilled not in material but in spiritual terms. The gospel of the Messiah whom Zerubbabel foreshadowed is not time-bound; it is universal in its scope and eternal in its relevance. Amid the upheavals of society, the changes and unrest among the nations, let us rejoice in the words of another Old Testament visionary:

I saw one like a human being coming with the clouds of heaven…
To him was given dominion and glory and kingship…
His dominion is an everlasting dominion that shall not pass away,
and his kingship is one that shall never be destroyed. (Daniel 7:13–14)

FURTHER READING

R.J. Coggins, *Haggai, Zechariah, Malachi*, Old Testament Guides, Sheffield Academic Press, 1987

Grace Emmerson, *Nahum to Malachi*, The People's Bible Commentary, BRF, 1998

REVELATION

Revelation 6:1—11:18

1 Introduction

You walk into a furniture store and see exactly what you are looking for, a box with 'Bedside Cabinet' written on it in large, friendly letters. As you journey home you imagine all the benefits of your new possession. However, having unpacked the flatpack and laid all the pieces on the floor you then come across a problem—you can't understand the assembly instructions. After a few hours of struggle you decide that this was never a bedside cabinet at all, but is in fact an abstract piece of sculpti-furniture, which expresses furniture-like themes and elements, but which is intentionally non-functional.

We can have a similar experience with Revelation. It claims to tell the story of 'what must soon take place' (1:1, 19; 4:1; 22:6) but the events it records proceed in a seemingly illogical order and involve characters who appear to have little to do with our everyday experience. In order to begin to understand Revelation, therefore, it is necessary to answer one basic question: Where and what is the story told by Revelation?

The straightforward answer to this question is that the story of 'what must soon take place' is contained within the scroll which only the Lamb may open (5:1). Unfortunately we must work a little harder to find out exactly where the contents of that scroll are recorded within the text of Revelation. Returning to the flat-pack analogy, let us say that we are principally interested in the raised surface that forms the top of the cabinet. To use that piece, however, we must work out how the rest of the elements of the kit work together to support that raised surface. By the end of the first week of readings we will have come some distance in establishing where the contents of the Lamb's scroll are directly revealed. The second and third weeks will focus on the story told by the scroll.

The interpretation of Revelation is a notoriously disputed field. The views presented in these notes are not representative of any consensus and should not, of course, be taken as anything more than the opinion of one particular scholar. My notes are based on the Revised Standard Version.

2 Seals and visions

Revelation 6:1–17

Chapters 1—5 of Revelation are *relatively* easy to understand. We begin, therefore, at chapter 6, just as things start to get complicated. Just prior to our reading John is caught up to heaven (4:1) and gains sight of the control room of the universe (chs. 4—5). In Revelation 5 an intense and universal focus of attention is brought to bear on the Lamb who was slain and the scroll that only he can open. It is the contents of this scroll that John's original hearers, and we his present readers, are on the edge of our seats to perceive. This is the scroll that contains the all-important story of 'what must take place after this' (4:1).

As Jesus the Lamb begins to break the seven seals on the scroll we can feel ourselves edging closer to gaining sight of its contents, but we cannot yet see them directly. A scroll sealed with seven seals is like a door bolted with seven bolts; you can't get through the door until *every* bolt is drawn. As each of the first six seals is broken a vision is seen. These accompanying visions act as trailers or foreshadowings of what the scroll will prove to contain when it is finally opened.

The first four visions are of messengers who ride to the four corners of the earth. Note that they are called out by each of the four Living Creatures from *each side* of the throne (6:1, 3, 5, 7; cf. 4:6) so they do not ride together as they are usually depicted. The actions that accompany the riders are prophetic of the type of thing that will appear when the Lamb's scroll is fully opened—judgment and disaster. These serve as warnings that give time for repentance and faithfulness to Christ.

The fifth and sixth visions indicate that the story within the scroll will include further martyrdoms (6:11) and the judgment and wrapping up of the whole of the old created order (6:12–17).

As a whole the six seal visions provide a kind of 'table of contents' of what the Lamb's scroll will prove to contain once it is fully opened. However, the scroll is still held shut by one seal, so we must wait before we can be privy to the full extent of its contents.

3 Security and worship

Revelation 7:1–4, 9–17

So far we know that the Lamb's scroll contains God's judgment on nations, even if we are still in suspense as to exactly how that judgment will be executed. The prospect of judgment raises an immediate and pressing question, 'What about us?' The universal language of Revelation 6 does not suggest that Christians will be exempt from what is about to happen, and the scroll is held shut by only one seal! Soon these things will come about.

The purpose of Revelation 7 is to show that, while God's faithful people are not immune from physical hardship, persecution and martyrdom, they are spiritually secure. What we have in this chapter is a kind of 'before and after' picture. The 144,000 represent the full complement of God's faithful people before the judgment begins. These are the 'true Jews' who follow Jesus the Messiah, that is, Christians.

The progress of the judgment is halted so that a spiritual seal of protection can be applied to this group (7:1–4). The great multitude (7:9–17) is a picture of the same group but at the *end* of the story. Thus, we see an almost identical scene in John's description of the new heaven and new earth (21:3–4). The purpose of this 'before and after' picture is to show that the spiritual protection given to Christ's followers prior to the judgment is effective throughout all that is to take place before the End. This was a reassurance to John's first hearers as it is a reassurance to us.

Revelation 7:9–17 gives us further details regarding the contents of the scroll. We gain a glimpse of the end of the story where those dressed in white robes feast in the presence of God. We can see here two features of our own Christian experience: the white robes of baptism and the heavenly feast of the Eucharist.

One of the outstanding features of Revelation is the way in which it presents the boundaries of heaven as embracing us as we worship God and take part in Holy Communion. Thus, in these verses we see characters who enjoy communion with God in heaven, but we also participate in that communion through our own baptism and through sharing in the feast of heaven that is extended to us in Holy Communion.

4 Silence

Revelation 8:1

In Revelation heaven is a future *and* a present reality. The worship in which we *will* participate is the worship in which we *do* participate now. As the Lamb opens the seventh seal there is silence in heaven for about half an hour.

Revelation would originally have been used in a liturgical setting. The silence in heaven would have been mirrored by a silence in the congregation who participate in the worship of heaven as they met together. The silence would not, of course, have been a blank one. This silence provides an opportunity for prayer and preparation. With the seventh seal broken the time of judgment is at hand. Now is a good opportunity to take time to pause ourselves as we reflect on the prospect of God's complete victory over, and judgment of, all that is evil.

In this verse we also encounter another important feature of Revelation, the presence of cliff-hanging instalment breaks. Imagine that you have been listening to Revelation 4—7 in the context of a church service. At the end of chapter 7 you seem to be just a hair's-breadth away from seeing the open scroll, and already you are putting together your own ideas as to what it will prove to contain. Before you are allowed to go on however, the performance stops. The service continues with a sharing of the bread and wine and the singing of hymns, in continuity with the singing, eating and drinking that is going on in heaven (7:15–17). However, to find out what happens next you must return to the church on the following Sunday to hear the next instalment, or in our case, wait until tomorrow for the next reading.

5 Trumpets

Revelation 8:1–6 (long reading 8:1—9:20)

Now, with the breaking of the final seal, we must surely be allowed direct access to the content of the Lamb's scroll, but we are not. We are kept in continued suspense by a set of trumpets which announce further partial details about the scroll.

The seven trumpets of Revelation have a particularly close relationship with the trumpets that announced the fall of Jericho. The Israelites circled the walls for six days (Joshua 6:3), and on the seventh day marched seven times around until the climactic blast and shout that brought the walls crashing down (Joshua 6:4–5). This suggests that all these announcements are leading up to the fall of a city.

The precise means by which the city will fall is intimated in the appearance of Apollyon/Abaddon (9:11) and the release of a barrier at the River Euphrates (9:14) so that a great army from the mysterious nether regions to the east can pour into the western lands. At the time John wrote, these were controlled by the Roman empire.

This picture represents an expansion on a tiny clue as to what the Lamb's scroll will contain that was provided in the first seal vision. The crowned, mounted archer of Revelation 6:2 should be seen as representing a king who comes to conquer from the lands beyond the River Euphrates. This is the case because mounted archers were used exclusively by armies from this region in the period we are considering. This king comes to conquer, and the mayhem he wreaks is indicated both in 6:3–8 and by the dire descriptions of war and distress to be found in Revelation 9.

The violence of Revelation is an issue to which we shall return. For the time being we must content ourselves with trying to understand what the text is saying, before we consider precisely why it says it. At this stage, therefore, we are beginning to piece together the idea that God's judgment is coming, and that the agent of that judgment is a king from the East. Our wait for final revelation of the scroll will continue until, as the angel says in 10:7, 'in the days when the seventh angel is to blow his trumpet, the mystery of God will be fulfilled, as he announced to his servants the prophets' (NRSV).

6 Security and vulnerability

Revelation 11:1–13 (long reading 10:1—11:18)

The blowing of the seventh announcing trumpet does not take place until 11:15. This indicates that everything that precedes 11:15 is designed to give us information about the contents of the Lamb's scroll, without actually directly revealing those contents.

In Revelation 10 we see John dress himself as an Old Testament prophet such as Daniel or Ezekiel. He takes a scroll given by an angel, eats it, and then speaks its contents in 11:1–13 (compare Ezekiel 2:8—3:3). The prophecy that John speaks in this guise represents a kind of potted version of the future predictions of the prophets of the past. The purpose of this small drama is to indicate that the Old Testament prophets announced, with partial completeness, the final scroll of Jesus Christ. We may expect, therefore, that 11:1–13 will once again give us some partial clues as to the kind of thing we shall eventually find in the Lamb's scroll.

From the trumpet visions we have gained a clear picture of impending disaster and judgment on those who do not have God's seal on their foreheads. The little scroll (11:1–13), on the other hand, focuses on the fate of God's faithful ones.

11:1–2 echoes the idea of the spiritual security amid the physical vulnerability of God's faithful people which we also saw in Revelation 7. Here the picture used is one of measuring the temple (a symbol of security) while allowing its outer courts to be trampled (indicating physical vulnerability).

This pattern of security and vulnerability is lived out in the career of the two witnesses. These characters, who represent God's faithful people, have the attributes of Elijah and Moses (11:6) and they testify through the period of tribulation or persecution which is variously represented as 1,260 days, 42 months or time, times and half a time (all equalling three and a half years).

The willingness of the witnesses to follow the example of Jesus is crucial to a central message of Revelation. They are faithful unto death (11:7), as he was; they are ridiculed and scorned (11.9–10), as he was; they are vindicated and raised (11:11–12), as he was; their faithful death and resurrection strikes a blow against the forces of evil (11:13), as his decisively did.

Guidelines

Through the course of Revelation 6:1—11:18 we are given a series of indirect insights into the contents of the Lamb's scroll. The six seal visions serve as an overall 'table of contents', the trumpet visions announce the coming bowl judgments (cf. Revelation 16) and the little scroll offers an 'Ezekiel's-eye-view' of the final events, which shall be fully revealed in the scroll of Jesus Christ.

It can almost feel as if the text is teasing the reader, persisting in holding back from revealing the full picture. However, this method of approach is far from gratuitous. What the text is trying to do is to help us to work it out for ourselves. Rather than simply lay down a map of future events, it encourages us to observe the world around us intelligently, thereby to understand how the universe works, and to act in the light of that understanding.

Revelation was addressed to particular communities at a particular time. This makes it possible that the foreshadowing images used in 6:1—11:18 relate to specific events in first-century history. For example, the sixth seal vision may be an allusion to the eruption of Vesuvius (AD79), or the martyrdom of the two witnesses may refer to the events of Nero's great persecution of Christians in Rome (AD64–65).

If this is the case, then the hearer is encouraged to envision history in the terms of a progressive cycle, so that future expectation is informed by observation of the past. Crucially in Revelation the past events of Christ's persecution, death and resurrection tell us something of what will happen in the future—on an even grander scale. This applies in both the negative and positive dimensions: there will be persecution as well as the general resurrection and the vindication of the righteous.

If Revelation is designed to encourage us to read the times, then what should we expect for our own future? As well as noting that there is a cycle in political history we must also recognize that the persecution of Christians is a recurrent feature of world history. Some of the churches addressed by Revelation probably felt that persecution was a million miles away (the Laodiceans for example), and it is tempting for western Christians to have the same perception. What Revelation insists on reminding us is that evil will always persist in trying to stamp out (by violent or more subtle means) that which is of Christ, and that only by following his pattern of life, even to death, can we participate in his victory over evil.

Revelation 12:1—17:18

1 Introduction

I began last week by suggesting that Revelation is similar to a flat-pack piece of furniture. We must discover the function of its constituent parts to understand how the whole works together to tell the story of 'what must soon take place'. One of the functions so far identified has been that of foreshadowing the contents of the scroll. These previews, such as the seal and trumpet visions, create an ideal circumstance for the performance of another type of function—the creation of cliff-hanging breaks between instalments. So, just as the final seal is about to be broken, the reading stops and the congregation must return next Sunday to discover what happens. Similarly, just as the final announcing trumpet is blown, the performance comes to a close and the suspense is carried over until the next week's reading.

The possibility that Revelation was designed to be read in instalments offers a new route to discovering where the elusive contents of the Lamb's scroll are revealed. When the text is divided into six units (starting at 1:1; 4:1; 8:1; 11:19; 15:5; and 19:11) it becomes apparent that some of the curious quirks in the flow of the text may be explained by its serial presentation.

For example, there are suspense-creating announcements prior to the cliff-hanging instalment breaks (as we have seen with the seal and trumpet visions, and which also occur in 14:6—15:4 and 19:5–9); the four middle instalments also close with a hymn which looks forward, at the end of the instalment, to God's final action; and each instalment opens with a new 'opening in heaven' which draws us closer to the final arrival of the Lord (in 19:11). More detail regarding this instalment theory may be found in my commentary on Revelation (published by Routledge, 1997).

By noting that 17:1—19:4 and 21:9—22.6 serve yet another function with respect to the contents of the scroll (namely, interpretative reviews of the preceding visions), it is possible to conclude that the different elements of Revelation work together to focus attention keenly on three particular passages: 12:1—14:5; 16:1–21; 19:11—21:8. I suggest that these passages contain the direct revelation of the contents of the Lamb's scroll, and it is to their interpretation that we now turn.

2 A child and Satan

Revelation 12:1–17

Every conflict has a history, and this is no less the case for the conflict between good and evil, Christ and Satan. Chapter 12 helps to fill in the background of the situation faced by Christians, both in John's time and our own.

The woman clothed with the sun appears to represent the faithful community of God's people, from whom the Messiah arises. (Mary is, of course, the epitome of those who belong to this community, but it is doubtful that she is the single referent behind this symbol.) That which comes from faithfulness to God is naturally abhorrent to Satan, and so he tries to destroy the child. However, in the very moment of the infant's apparently inevitable destruction, he is caught up to the throne of God. Then, because of Christ's exaltation it is possible for Michael to evict Satan from heaven.

One of the questions raised by this passage is, Why did Satan's eviction have to wait until the death and resurrection of Christ? A clue to a possible answer may lie in the description of Satan as 'the accuser, who accuses [our comrades] day and night before our God' (12:10). Thus it is possible that Satan sought the death penalty for each human being by inexorably pointing out their failure to keep God's law. This tactic could not work in the case of Jesus, however, and so Satan's falsity was exposed.

In the battle against evil, Revelation consistently appeals to its hearers to bear unjust suffering, even unto death, so as to expose the enemy for who and what he is (12:11). The early Christians took this call entirely seriously and thereby undermined even the might of the Roman empire. Movements of passive resistance in more recent times have also been successful in exposing and defeating evil regimes. In the fight against evil, whether on a large or small scale, a genuine and persistent holiness is perhaps our sharpest weapon.

3 A beastly head

Revelation 13:1–10, 18

Having been cast down to earth the dragon focuses his attack on the children of the woman, the Christian community. Standing on the shore of the sea (12:18) he calls forth the agent by which he will bring about their persecution—the beast from the sea (13:1). The water has not dripped from this extraordinary monster before its identity as a political animal is revealed. It appears as a composite of the four beasts seen by Daniel.

These beasts were political empires, and so it is natural to identify the beast of Revelation with a political empire. We should be careful, however, of making the easy assumption that John always refers to the entire Roman empire whenever he mentions the beast. Indeed, after 13:2 the image that fills John's lens is not the beast in its entirety but *one* of its heads only; the one with the mortal wound. Thus the beast is given a mouth (only one) to utter blasphemous names (13:5) and it reigns for 42 months (13:5), a very short period if the Roman empire as a whole is referred to here.

An additional indication that not all of the heads of the beast, as described in 13:1–2, are truly 'beastly' may be found in 17:10–11. Here we are told that one of the seven heads (representing Roman emperors) *is living* at the time of writing, and yet the beast 'is not'. This means that the beast who 'was, and is not, and is to ascend from the bottomless pit' (17:8) must be *one* of the seven heads who has reigned in the past, is currently absent, but who is expected to reappear at some future date (cf. 17:11).

The first-century Roman emperor who fits Revelation's description of the beastly head most completely is Nero. Although Nero committed suicide in AD68, a widespread myth held that he had escaped to the East, beyond Euphrates, and was gathering an army with which to recapture his empire. This explains the beastly head's recovery from a mortal wound (13:3) and his identity as the king who was, is not, and is to come (17:8–11). Nero's name also provides the most satisfactory interpretation of the number 666 (see the commentaries). Nero is also an obvious candidate for the antichristian beast in that he initiated the first persecution of Christians, after the burning of Rome in AD64.

4 A second beast

Revelation 13:11–17

The identification of the beast with Nero has important implications for the interpretation of the figure behind the second beast (also described as the 'false prophet' in 16:13). It is highly unlikely that the Roman imperial cult (the body usually identified with the second beast) would have promoted the worship of Nero, since no sitting emperor could have welcomed the prospect of the renegade's return.

However, as Richard Bauckham writes in his *Climax of Prophecy* (pp. 449–50):

For much of the population of the eastern provinces of the empire it seems… that Nero's return was not merely the object of expectation but an object of eager hope. The philhellene emperor, friendly to the Parthians, had acquired the mythic image of a messianic saviour figure, who would wreak the vengeance of the east on the west and re-establish the rule of the east'.

It is possible, therefore, that the second beast represents a local group in Asia Minor who looked forward to Nero's return.

Yet, this raises the question, Then why should this figure loom so large on John's horizon? A possible explanation would be that the persons behind the second beast were in fact members of John's own congregations. The second beast has horns like a lamb (13:11), which may suggest that it masquerades as a Christian, and the use of the term 'false prophet' (16:13) was very much more commonly used to describe a 'Christian' rather than a pagan prophet. I believe, therefore, that Jezebel (2:20-24) and Balaam (2:14) are the figures behind the second beast. These two persons, designated by their nicknames as false prophets, were evidently leading their congregations astray. Their encouragement of the eating of food sacrificed to idols (2:13, 20) may indicate a tug of allegiance between the participation at the Lord's supper (cf. 3:20) and sharing in pagan feasts.

Perhaps the most important feature of the second beast, whatever its precise identity, is that it had the appearance of innocence, symbolized by its two lamb-like horns. John warns us that appearances can be deceptive. We may think that we are following Christ when we follow a widespread 'Christian' practice but the ultimate test of all these things is whether they promote an undivided allegiance to Christ and conformity with the way of Christ.

5 Two armies

Revelation 14:1–5 (long reading 14:1—15:4)

The beast conquers the saints (13:7) and the second beast causes those who will not worship the beast's image to be slain (13:15). But what is the ultimate fate of these martyrs? In 14:1–5 the text pulls back to take in a wider perspective and reveals that those who were 'conquered' and slain have in fact followed the pattern of their Lord and, because of their faithful death, have joined the heavenly throng. Specifically, they join an army that is ranged in opposition against the forces of Satan. The evil army will ultimately gather on 'Mount Megiddo', or Armageddon as it is more commonly known (cf. 16:13–16). The contrast between these two armies is so great as to make the prospect of any ensuing conflict almost farcical. The 144,000 have no armour, being dressed only in white robes, and they have no visible weapons beside their own holiness. However, in the battle between good and evil, holiness is the only truly effective weapon and defence.

Because of the imperfections of our age it is tempting to resign ourselves to the idea that, in the moral sphere, nothing is truly black and white, and that everything is just one shade of grey or another. This is an attractive position from a pragmatic point of view, but it is one that disables the fight against evil. It is not possible for Christians to condemn a practice in which they are also engaged; the charge of hypocrisy will always instantly undermine our efforts. By contrast, Christ's stand against evil is unassailable because of his holiness; inasmuch as we follow him our efforts can also be effective.

After 14:5 the contents of the Lamb's scroll are put aside for a period during which a further set of announcements are issued (14:6–20). Together with the appearance of the seven bowl angels (15:1), these announcements look forward to the judgment of Babylon (Rome) for its part in the persecution of Christians in AD64–65. By this means, suspense is created through the course of 14:6—15:4 which leads up to a cliff-hanging instalment break immediately after 15:4.

6 The harlot and the beast

Revelation 17:1–18 (long reading 15:5—17:18)

At the beginning of the fifth instalment (15:5—19:10) the bowl angels, which were seen at the end of the fourth instalment (12:19—15:4), reappear. These angels then pour out their judgments through the course of chapter 16. At the beginning of chapter 17 one of the bowl angels offers an interpretative review of the preceding judgments. This passage is difficult to follow but it does provide crucial clues regarding the shape and significance of the central section of the Lamb's scroll.

The angel begins by showing John the whore who rides upon the beast. Various clues (e.g. 'the seven heads are seven mountains' [17:9] and 'the woman that you saw is the great city…' [17:18]) identify the harlot as the city of Rome. This woman is depicted in 17:6 as 'drunk with the blood of the saints and the blood of the martyrs of Jesus'. This suggests that the inhabitants of Rome are under judgment because of their participation in the persecution initiated by Nero after the burning of Rome in AD64.

The means of Rome's judgment is, ironically, at the hands of the returning Nero himself. Thus, the beast who reigned in the past will come again to recapture his empire (17:8, 11) with the help of the 'ten horns' (17:12)—a possible reference to Nero's Parthian allies. Revelation 17:16 offers the clearest description of these events. It says that ten horns (the Parthian rulers) will unite with the beast (the returning Nero) and will make the harlot (the city of Rome) desolate, naked, devoured and burned. 'For one hour' (17:12)—that is, a very short time—Nero and his allies will have supremacy. However, when they make war on the Lamb they shall be conquered (17:14).

The events described in this passage did not come about as John describes them. This may be because my interpretation is incorrect, or it may be because he is doing something more than offering straightforward future prediction. Some of John's opponents seemed to believe that either Rome or Nero would be supreme in the future. In response Revelation states that, whatever the future predictions of others, the ultimate end of history must always rest in the final victory of Christ.

Guidelines

Revelation is about seeing. John is taken up to heaven (4:1) from where he can see events on earth in a broader perspective and with more penetrating insight. His heavenly viewpoint enlarges his vision so that he can see the earthly power of Rome, or Nero, alongside the final victory of Christ and the sovereignty of God Almighty. John's new vantage point also allows him to distinguish between the fake and the real, even though, on the surface, they appear almost identical.

For example, the beast with the mortal wound (13:3) is distinguished from the slain Lamb (5:6); the beast who was, and is not, and is to come (17:8) is distinguished from the God who was, is, and is to come (1:8); the two witnesses who faithfully prophesy (11:6) are distinguished from the two-horned beast which prophesies falsely (13:15); the army on Mount Zion who bear the seal of God (14:1) are distinguished from the army on Mount Megiddo who bear the mark of the beast.

Revelation is about seeing the future, but by a very particular method. How things are in the present has a profound effect on how they will be in the future. So, for example, knowing that army A is very much stronger than army B allows the prediction that army A will win a future conflict. John's vision shows him that Christ is eternally victorious over evil through his faithful death and resurrection. This aspect of present reality means that any prediction of future events must always end with Christ's ultimate victory. This knowledge allows John to see beyond any vision of the future that his opponents might offer, such as the return of Nero as a messianic saviour. Thus, Revelation allows for the possibility of Nero's return but responds by insisting that such a return could never be the end of the story. Christ is eternally victorious over evil.

In the twenty-first century we still use our understanding of the present to predict how the future will turn out. It may be that we believe that the USA will always be a superpower, or that Islam will invade the world, or that liberal capitalism will rescue the world from every other political system. Revelation's response to all such predictions is that there is no power that can ever overturn the victory of Jesus Christ, so put your trust in nothing else.

Revelation 19:1—22:21

1 A wedding banquet

Revelation 19:1–10

After the destruction of Babylon there is great rejoicing. It can be hard for us to know quite what to make of passages like this: we are, after all, taught to love our enemies. One observation to bear in mind, however, is that salvation from oppression and persecution can only be achieved through the just judgment of the oppressor. We might feel differently about these scenes of destruction if we belonged to a persecuted Christian community that was crying out for vindication. It is also worth bearing in mind that Christians in the West live within an economic system that benefits from the oppression of people in developing countries. Does this fact contribute in some part to our discomfort?

Revelation 19:1–10 is the final passage of the text's fifth instalment (15:5—19:10) and, in common with those passages which close the other five instalments, an element of suspense is created by the announcement of a future event; in this case the wedding supper of the Lamb. This event represents an important resolution of tension, but its description is held off until the next and final instalment.

In some branches of Christianity the idea that heaven will be like a wedding supper is not commonly taught. However, the prospect of a messianic banquet at the end of all things was a common and vivid image of future hope in the time of Jesus. We can see a reference to this belief when a dinner guest says to Jesus, 'Blessed is anyone who will eat bread in the kingdom of God!' (Luke 14:15; cf. also Psalm 23; Matthew 8:11 and Luke 13:29). Thus we will indeed be blessed, as Revelation 19:9 says, if we are invited to the marriage supper of the Lamb. The amazing thing is that we are invited, and can begin to experience a foretaste of that heavenly meal when we share the Eucharist. As we gather to worship God, we join with those in heaven who also worship him. As we eat the heavenly meal that only Christ has made available to us we join with those in heaven who also sit at his table. As we worship, the boundaries of heaven embrace us.

2 The Rider

Revelation 19:11–21

The warrior Messiah who here bursts upon the scene is Jesus, the same character who was earlier portrayed as an innocent Lamb (5:6) and as a newborn baby (12:5). He is followed by an army of white-robed figures who, earlier in the story, were portrayed as the helpless victims of the beast (13:7), and who, following their executions, have been gathering on Mount Zion (14:1–5). Once again Revelation invites us to see beyond appearances to apprehend an underlying spiritual reality. Holiness, which appears so weak, is in fact the power that defeats evil however mighty its forces may seem.

The multiple description of the Rider provides more detail as to the source of his might and the means of his impending victory. Because he is faithful and true, he is able to detect the sometimes subtle divide between good and evil, and to condemn evil without condemning himself. His flaming eyes suggest penetrating insight into the reality behind all things. His multiple crowns convey his universal sovereignty, even over the dragon with seven crowns (12:3) and the beast with ten crowns (13:1). His unknowable name (19:12) is another symbol of his sovereignty; he cannot be contained within human categories. His blood-soaked robe (19:13) has provoked various interpretations. It may be the blood of his enemies, but I think it is more likely the blood of his own sacrifice (which makes white the robes of the saints in 7:14). In true Johannine style he is also named as the Word of God (19:13). This name makes us think back to Genesis 1; this Rider is the agent by which God effects the new creation.

The scenes of judgment that follow are bloody and violent (19:15–21). The Messiah sounds more like a ruthless dictator than a loving saviour. What are we to make of these scenes? A principle that must be borne in mind with this passage, and others like it, is that Revelation deals in spiritual rather than physical realities. With perfect spiritual eyesight Christ is able to detect evil and utterly destroy it. That is an outcome that can genuinely be received with rejoicing, even as we seek the death of that which is evil within ourselves.

3 End-time events

Revelation 20:1–6

Those who believe that Revelation provides a map of the end must try to fit Christ's thousand-year reign into a suitable sequence of events, alongside the tribulation (a final persecution of God's faithful people), the parousia (the Messiah's return) and the rapture (when the saints are caught up to meet Christ in the air; cf. 1 Thessalonians 4:17). The issue of the order in which these events may be expected to occur is complicated by the curious structure of Revelation because, reading from start to finish, it doesn't seem to follow a linear progression. This introduces the possibility that the story-line presented in chapters 19 and 20 is not meant to be taken sequentially. This point is sometimes used to justify the theory that the rapture will take place before the tribulation. This is an attractive idea in that it allows Christians to escape the coming persecution, but it is strongly at odds with the thrust of Revelation.

Given that Revelation so firmly promotes the need for faithfulness through persecution, it seems preferable, to me at least, not to reorder the sequence of 19:11—21:8. On this understanding the white-robed army of 19:14 are those who have been through the tribulation and, because of their faithfulness unto death, have been caught up to join the army of martyrs (seen gathering on Mount Zion in 14:1–5), and which ultimately follows the Messiah at his coming (19:14). After the imprisonment of Satan, this army then reigns with Jesus on earth for a 'messianic age' of a thousand years.

This may be the most straightforward way of reading the text, but is it meant to be taken literally? This is a difficult question to answer. However, it may be significant that some Jews of the period believed in a future 'messianic age', such as the 400-year earthly bliss mentioned in 4 Ezra 7:28 (this book is included in the Apocrypha, sometimes entitled 2 Esdras). It is possible, therefore, that Revelation is here primarily concerned to indicate that the ones who will inherit God's promises are those who belong to the true Israel. Revelation is in no doubt as to the definition of this group—it is those who belong to Jesus Christ, the Lion of Judah and Root of David (5:5).

4 Universal victory

Revelation 20:7–15

Thus far the story of 'what must soon take place' has largely focused on two of Satan's allies and agents, the beast (Nero?) and the false prophet (Jezebel and Balaam?). These figures may have loomed large on the horizon viewed by John's churches, but they do not encompass the embodiment of evil in every time and place.

One of the central themes of Revelation is that God and his Christ will ultimately triumph over all that is evil. The universality of that victory, beyond the local issue of Jezebel and the rest (19:20), is expressed using the symbol of Gog and Magog. These names first appear in Ezekiel 38—39, where Gog is a person and Magog is his kingdom. By the time these names are used in Revelation, however, they serve as a symbol for all the ancient enemies of God's faithful people, across the dimensions of time and space.

The picture painted here, therefore, is of Satan gathering everyone he can possibly muster for a final assault on Christ and his faithful ones. They swarm across the land in countless numbers (20:8) and seem sure to swallow the city of the just (20:9). But even these last reinforcements are swiftly defeated along with Satan himself (20:9b–10). Revelation 20:10 (and 14:11) provide what is probably the strongest biblical evidence for the view that hell is a place of ever-lasting torment. Whether or not these verses should be interpreted literally, the crucial property of the lake of fire is that it is a place of no return. Evil can never escape from it.

For those of us who have been brought up to believe in 'justification by faith alone', the scene of final judgment (20:11–15) can feel uncomfortable because judgment is according to what has been done. However, there is nothing in this vision that is at odds with the teaching of Paul. He argued that we are made righteous (justified) as a result of our faith in Christ. That is to say that righteousness is a real effect of membership of Christ, and of being directed by his Spirit. We are not saved by believing in 'justification by faith', but by belonging to the one who, when we belong to him alone, causes us to act righteously.

5 Heavenly speech

Revelation 21:1–8 (long reading 21:1—22:5)
Revelation 21:1–8 presents the dénouement of the story of 'what must soon take place'. Here is the final resolution of the many

tensions within the text. Finally, the battle with evil is completed.

At the centre of Revelation's vision of heaven is the idea of restoration. Earth and heaven are renewed because they are freed from the destructive effects of sin. God is able to dwell with his people again because his holiness no longer separates them from him. The bride and her husband are no longer kept apart. They are, at last, able to become one.

Integral to John's vision of heaven as a place of restoration is his understanding of it as a place of purity. The significance of the speech at 21:5–8 cannot be underestimated. The One on the throne has been an overarching presence throughout the whole of the main vision cycle (from 4:1 onwards), but he does not speak until now. His words arrest the hearer's attention and encapsulate the message of Revelation.

First, in the Alpha and Omega saying (21:6), they express the sovereignty of God. This fact stands like an ever-present arc across the span of Revelation. There can be no course of history that does not ultimately end in God, its originator.

Second, there is the promise of a fully restored relationship with God for those who conquer (21:6b–7). As we have seen, conquering is not achieved by physical violence. Rather, it is won by following the pattern of Jesus, the one who was faithful unto death.

Third, there is the assurance that those who do not follow the pattern of Christ (in the power of the Holy Spirit) cannot take part in the heavenly End (21:8). This last verse sits uneasily with the preceding seven, and is commonly omitted when this passage is read in church or at funeral services. This omission is understandable because the message of 21:8 seems harsh and unforgiving. Unfortunately, one of the points Revelation persists in making is the hard fact that the suffering of the innocent will never be brought to an end until its causes are confronted and destroyed.

6 Coming soon

Revelation 22:6–21

The great cycle of heavenly visions comes to a close at 22:7 and in 22:6 an angel reflects on all that has gone before. He notes that the story of 'what must soon take place' (promised in 1:1, 19 and 4:1), has now been revealed. The story that has been told consists of the further persecution of God's people, the punishment of the persecutors and the vindication of the persecuted.

As the text looks back on all that has gone before it also looks forward to the future realization of all that has been predicted. Thus, in 22:7, the Christ who is to be the agent of perfectly just judgment, and thereby the agent of punishment as well as vindication, announces that he is coming soon. This is like a cup of cold water in the face of the reader.

For the last few chapters we have been caught up in a visionary world that seems a million miles from our everyday experience. In the announcement of 22:7, however, we are invited to recall that the world inside the text is by no means removed from the world in which we live our day-to-day lives. When the Lord arrives in our flesh-and-blood reality, then the pattern of conflict and conquest described in 19:11—20:15 may be expected actually to happen.

Revelation repeatedly claims that these things will happen 'soon'. This text was written more than nineteen hundred years ago, so what are we to make of this expectation of imminence? An explanation for this apparent conflict may perhaps be found in 22:20. Here the congregation respond to Christ's acclamation, 'Surely I am coming soon' with the response, 'Amen. Come, Lord Jesus'.

The term used here is *Maranatha* (expressed in Greek), a term also used to close a similar set of acclamations in a eucharistic prayer to be found in the Didache. (The Didache is a first-century Christian manual whose eucharistic material predates, in my opinion, the book of Revelation.) This invites the possibility that we can create an experience of the End in our own time. That is to say, we can invite Christ into our midst, we can accept him as our Lord, and so experience a foretaste of his final breaking into history and his final victory.

Guidelines

Having provided a new understanding of reality, Revelation calls for a response to what has been seen. The response that is required is exclusive allegiance to Christ and to the way of Christ. The act which signifies the acceptance of this call is the reception of the bread and wine at Holy Communion. This is the case because in eating the bread and wine we identify with Christ in his death; we recognize that our life outside Christ must die. In this act we also identify with Christ in his risen life; we become members of his body and so are directed by his Spirit, just as the limbs of a body are directed by the head.

At the end of each instalment, Revelation offers its audience the opportunity to make this response of allegiance to Christ. For example, at the end of the first instalment (1:1—3:22,) he offers to come in and eat with the Laodiceans, and they with him (3:20). This offer is not merely a sign of friendship, it is an invitation to declare exclusive loyalty to Christ.

Revelation was first addressed to communities where other feasts were available; it appears that Jezebel and Balaam were teaching that it was permitted to eat at Christ's table and at the table of idols (2:14, 20). In the West we are not surrounded by pagan feasts as such, but we have plenty of opportunity to buy into systems and policies that are opposed to Christ. Financial pressures in particular can cause us to make allegiances that are incompatible with membership of Christ (cf. 13:16–17). However, Revelation teaches that such divided loyalties are not possible.

Participation in Christ is not only participation in the Christ who suffered and died. It is also membership of the one who is raised. Our sharing of the bread and wine of the Eucharist is also a sharing in a foretaste of the messianic banquet, the marriage supper of the Lamb. This means that our life and worship together is in continuity with the life and worship of heaven, just as our eating is in continuity with that heavenly meal. When strangers join us, therefore, they should find a colony of heaven, a shop window of the hope that we profess. Herein lies a considerable, and joyous, challenge.

RUTH

The little book of Ruth is tucked away between two long books, Judges and Samuel, both of them with many tales of violence and deceit. Ruth, in contrast, is an enchanting tale of success after distress, of fulfilment after bereavement. Here are two women, Ruth and Naomi, of independent mind who manage their own lives within a patriarchal society, even though ultimately they are dependent on a man, Boaz, for protection.

Coming immediately after the book of Judges, it counterbalances the degradation of women in the horrific events of Judges 19 and 21, with its tale of loyalty and courage, and of mutual respect between man and woman. Only one other Old Testament book, Esther, bears a woman's name. It is sometimes suggested that Ruth, in its sensitivity, was written by a woman but this is purely speculative. Certainly it gives centre-stage mainly to two women. Old Testament women often remain in the shadows, but here, in Ruth herself, is a woman of flesh and blood, a real woman, quick to size up a situation and to take advantage of it!

The apparently artless narrative is skilfully structured. There is humour, too, as we shall see in our readings. Only twice does the Lord intervene directly as events unfold, but the whole narrative is shot through with strong religious commitment. It is pre-eminently a story of faithful devotion both human and divine.

The story is set in the pre-monarchic era of the Judges, a time of anarchy and lawlessness (Judges 21:25), but the opening verse and the explanatory note in 4:7 make it clear that it was written at a later date. Indeed the end of the book reaches into David's time.

The notes are based mainly on the NRSV. Other translations are referred to occasionally.

1 Refugee in an alien land

Ruth 1:1–14

The story starts with a surprise, a refugee family from Bethlehem seeking safety in Moab, a foreign country and an alien one (Deuteronomy 23:3). For the book's first readers, the marriage to Moabite wives would be still more startling. Wasn't it Moabite women who led Israel into disaster on the way to the promised land (Numbers 25:1–3)? Clearly this story is going to be unconventional.

At first sight it seems a hopeless story with no future, a woman without husband and sons, living far from home in a foreign land with two Moabite daughters-in-law! But, as the story unfolds, God is a God of surprises. The story starts in Moab and ends in Bethlehem; it starts with bereavement and ends in blessing. For the Lord takes the initiative (v. 6), the first of his two direct interventions in this human tale. And Naomi, too, takes action: 'she heard… so she set out…'

From the beginning Naomi's character is ambiguous. She is courageous yet despairing, starting towards her future yet denying its possibility. She is grateful to her daughters-in-law (v. 8) and concerned for their vulnerability in a society where only marriage provided real security. Yet there may be self-pity too: 'It has been far more bitter for me than for you' (v. 13 NRSV). The Hebrew, however, is ambiguous and may express affectionate concern: 'It is exceedingly bitter to me for your sake' (RSV). The first inkling of Ruth's character with its devoted loyalty and firm resolve comes in verse 14, characteristics maintained consistently throughout the story.

Naomi attributes both blessing and disaster to the Lord, but note there is no suggestion that the latter is regarded as punitive.

2 Journey into the unknown

Ruth 1:15–22

Verse 14 gave the first hint of Ruth's commitment to Naomi. She clung (*dabaq*) to her, the word used in Genesis 2:24 of the commitment of man to wife. Ruth is a woman of independent mind. To follow what someone else does, in this case her sister-in-law, is not Ruth's way.

In probably the best-known words in the book she expresses unreserved, lifelong devotion, relegating to the past her homeland and her ancestral faith. This commitment is reminiscent in its expression of the covenant made between God and Israel at Sinai (Leviticus 26:12). But still the ambiguity of Naomi's character remains. Is her silence (v. 18) significant? It is difficult to say. Certainly it is dis-appointing to find no warm, affectionate response to Ruth's promise.

Ruth's willingness to leave her past behind reminds us of Abraham who went out 'not knowing where he was going' (Hebrews 11:8). Ruth, at least, knew that they were heading for Bethlehem. But Abraham had God's promise of a future: 'I will bless you, and make your name great' (Genesis 12:2). Ruth made her choice with no divine promise and no sign of future blessing. Yet she knew she was journeying with God. Her commitment was total, not to familiar places, to home and security, but to a person, to Naomi and to Naomi's God.

Now back in Bethlehem where the Lord had given his people food (*lehem*, v. 6), Naomi is full of self-pity: 'don't call me Naomi [pleasant] but Mara [bitter]'. What of gratitude due to the Lord and to Ruth? A warning, perhaps, what lack of thanksgiving can do to the soul. Naomi's bitterness startles the reader. Did she go away *full*, fleeing as a starving refugee to an alien land? Did she come back *empty*, surrounded as she was by Ruth's devotion and enabled to share in the Lord's provision?

The chapter which began with famine ends with harvest. Now we have the first emphasis on Ruth as foreigner. Ruth the Moabite is not yet recognized as part of the community.

3 'Work-fare'—and more!

Ruth 2:1–13

The story takes an unexpected turn. Naomi is not after all alone. She has a wealthy, influential relative (the Hebrew words convey the idea of strength too) on her husband's side, a comment preparing us for the story's unfolding. Now it is not Naomi but Ruth who is a widow in a foreign country, and she doesn't know of the wealthy relative. She claims the right of the poor to glean in the fields (Leviticus 19:10), a kind of 'work-fare', and hard work it was. Among the unfenced strips of land belonging to various owners, she came by chance (v. 3) to Boaz's land. But this storyteller knows of no conflict between chance from the human perspective and Yahweh's provision.

It is a story of courtesy. Ruth asks Naomi's permission to go out to glean (v. 2); Boaz greets the reapers with a traditional greeting (Psalm 129:8). The patriarchal assumptions of society are apparent in Boaz's question (v. 5), not 'Who is this girl?' but 'To whom does she belong?' The servant identifies Ruth by her foreign origins. Boaz's character starts to unfold. He gives Ruth fatherly advice: 'Keep close to my young women', and 'keep your eyes on the field'! Despite the formality and courtesy we noted, this is a rough society. Ruth is young, and Boaz is realistic. He is kindly, too, sparing Ruth the effort of drawing water for herself in the heat. She is to have free access to the large water pots, possibly goatskins.

Ruth is a foreigner, a newcomer with no legal rights of protection, unlike the 'resident alien' protected by law and recognized as part of the community. But stranger though she is, Ruth is not unknown to Boaz. Rumour has been rife. He knows of her loyalty and courage. Her adventurous spirit he has yet to discover!

With verse 12 we find the theme of reward. Of this Boaz himself eventually becomes the agent, a point worth bearing in mind when we pray for others. The Hebrew text highlights this by a play on words. Boaz, in terms reminiscent of the psalms (e.g. 36:7 and 57:1), wishes Ruth a reward from the Lord 'under whose wings (*kanaph*) you have come for refuge'. It is under Boaz's cloak (*kanaph*; literally 'skirt') that she finds refuge (3:9). The expression 'you have spoken kindly' (Hebrew 'to the heart'), used of wooing in Hosea 2:14, may hint at the way the story is unfolding.

4 Mother-in-law and daughter-in-law

Ruth 2:14–23

From being an outsider, Ruth is welcomed into the group by Boaz, a man not of kind words only but of unstinting generosity. There is bread, wine and popcorn for Ruth to share, and more than enough, surely a reflection of the Lord's provision (Psalm 81:10), and special help with her gleaning besides. Ruth's character, too, is consistent both in her industrious activity and in her concern for Naomi. And all the time the older woman is busy matchmaking none too subtly behind the scenes!

The interplay of mother-in-law and daughter-in-law is fascinating. The wise older woman is concerned for her daughter-in-law's reputation. Letting her into the secret of Boaz's identity, Naomi uses the technical term *goel*, 'redeemer' (Leviticus 25:25: applied to the Lord in Job 19:25: 'I know that my Redeemer lives'). Here is security for the future. Naomi attributes it to the Lord's doing who 'always keeps his promises to the living and the dead' (v. 20 GNB).

But Ruth, the young widow, is lively and adventurous. Here is a humorous touch. Ruth quotes Boaz: he said 'Stay close by my servants (young men).' But Boaz had said, 'Keep close to my young women' (2:8). Ruth is deliberately mischievous, and Naomi knows it. She is a real human being, not a cardboard cut-out. And so Naomi is ready with a motherly warning: 'It is better... that you go out with his young women.' Clearly Ruth's use of the masculine was not accidental!

Ruth beats out on the spot with a stick what she has gleaned, a practice illustrated in the story of Gideon (Judges 6:11). The weight of an ephah is uncertain, possibly 25 kilos, but clearly not too much for Ruth to carry.

Chapter 1 began with famine and ended with harvest. Chapter 2 concludes with the ending of the corn harvest. Immediate needs have been satisfied, but what of the future? Already a hint has been given of longer term security, hence the intrigue of the following scene.

5 Naomi's matchmaking!

Ruth 3:1–18

In contrast to the previous scene, this is a private chapter. The three main characters are involved. Naomi hatches the plan, Ruth puts it into effect and Boaz is not slow to respond. Ruth is resourceful, only in the shadows (literally) when she startles Boaz in the darkness!

Naomi, so observant of convention in safeguarding Ruth's honour, now plans a thoroughly unconventional scheme to secure her own and Ruth's future. Again Ruth's mischievous streak breaks out. She sounds submissively obedient (v. 5) but acts resourcefully. Naomi said, '[Boaz] will tell you what to do' (v. 4). In the event Ruth tells Boaz what to do (v. 9)! The preparations for her meeting with Boaz resemble those of a bride, and here's a homely touch; Naomi instructs her to wait until he has finished his meal and his wine. A thread of humour certainly runs through this story.

Verses 7–14 are tantalizingly obscure, no doubt deliberately so, for the author is a sophisticated storyteller. There are sexual overtones, that is all one can say. A threshing floor with its piles of grain afforded privacy (hence a place to which prostitutes resorted: Hosea 9:1). Ruth's request, 'Spread your skirt (*kanaph*) over your maidservant' (RSV), is taken in the Good News Bible as an explicit proposal of marriage by Ruth, 'Please marry me.' Her action is unconventional but clearly not scandalous, since Boaz, as he blesses her, calls her 'a worthy woman' (the term used of the ideal wife in Proverbs 31:10). But the conventions must be observed, hence the request for secrecy.

Ruth's action must be seen in its ancient context, motivated by the fact that Boaz is not a stranger but a *goel* ('one with the right to redeem' NRSV footnote). The Old Testament nowhere specifies marriage as a *goel*'s responsibility but general care for a poor family member including restoration of property (Leviticus 25:25,47–49). Now comes a further twist in the story, something of which Naomi was apparently unaware. There is a closer relative than Boaz and on him the responsibility rests in the first instance.

The recurring theme of emptiness and fullness continues here. Ruth doesn't return home empty-handed (v. 17). The present is safeguarded for Naomi and Ruth, the prelude to the securing of the future.

6 The future is born

Ruth 4:1–21

After the intimacy of the previous chapter, this scene takes place entirely in public hence, in that patriarchal society, all the participants are men. Ruth's nearer relative, hinted at in 3:12, appears on the scene, unnamed, a shadowy figure. (The Hebrew refers to him as 'so and so', *peloni almoni*!) The area inside the city gate was the traditional place for business dealings (see Proverbs 31:23). This is a legal transaction. Naomi is selling her dead husband's land and the next of kin has first option on it.

But here is something of a mystery: Why, if Naomi owned land, were she and Ruth so poor as to glean in others' fields? The next of kin agrees to purchase the land—until he hears of Ruth and marriage. So far he had known only of Naomi, an older widow. The young widow presents a problem: a child of Ruth's would inherit the land and thus disadvantage his own family.

Now the way is open for Boaz to marry Ruth. The ritual of removing the sandal (vv. 7–8) is simply a confirmation of the transaction. No shame is attached to it as in the humiliating ritual of Deuteronomy 25:5–10 which concerns dereliction of duty with regard to the obligation to marry a dead brother's widow to maintain his family (levirate marriage).

Ruth's relationship with Boaz, which began furtively and unconventionally, must be ratified publicly and formally. There is nothing shifty or scandalous about their marriage. Ruth, still the outsider in verses 5 and 10, becomes part of Israel. She is likened to Rachel and Leah, Jacob's wives, mothers of the twelve tribes, and to Tamar, a famous outsider who in even more unconventional manner gave birth to a future for a line facing extinction (Genesis 38). In Matthew's Gospel both Tamar (1:3) and Ruth (1:5) are included in the genealogy of Jesus, the Messiah.

Now for the second time Yahweh explicitly intervenes (v. 13). Ruth fades into the background, scarcely more than a surrogate mother for Naomi's child (vv. 14–16). But here at last is the sole mention of 'love' in what is often described as a love story: the love of daughter-in-law for mother-in-law. In this love the sadness of past days is obliterated. At last Ruth is no longer called 'the Moabite'.

We have caught glimpses of the patriarchal assumptions of ancient Israelite society. Women needed a male protector, and such this new male child will become. Yet the women's insight (v. 15) sets the importance of sons in perspective. The love of this foreign young woman, related to Naomi only by marriage, is of supreme value. The women who understood Naomi's distress (1:19–21) now share her joy, and it is they (exceptionally) who name the child. Yet, despite this, the concluding genealogy is unashamedly male. How surprising, then, that the book bears Ruth's name!

This story which started with tragic names, three men dying in a foreign land, ends with the names of those through whom the future was secured, not for a single, obscure family but for the nation Israel and for all the world, for of this line the promised Messiah was born: 'a light for revelation to the Gentiles and for glory to your people Israel' (Luke 2:32).

The book of Judges ends in anarchy: 'all the people did what was right in their own eyes'. The book of Ruth ends with David of whose line came the King offering peace to the *world*. May his kingdom come!

Guidelines

Ruth is a story to treasure. It belongs to domestic life, to a family circle. It points us to a God who intervenes in human life, not in spectacular, dramatic events but in everyday sorrows and joys. Always, whatever the past, he is God of the future, bringing hope out of despair, new life after loss.

We have had a glimpse into an ancient patriarchal society where the voice of women often remained unheard. This little book has given a fresh perspective. The focus has been mainly on two women, resourceful, loyal and loving through whom in the end the world's hope, the child Immanuel, was born. For this fresh perspective, if for no other, the book of Ruth should be treasured.

FURTHER READING

R.L. Hubbard, *The Book of Ruth*, The New International Commentary on the Old Testament, Eerdmans, 1988

Katrina Larkin, *Ruth and Esther*, Old Testament Guides, Sheffield Academic Press, 1996

Ellen van Wolde, *Ruth and Naomi*, SCM Press, 1997

THE HOSPITABLE KINGDOM

As I write, our possessions are strewn around the floor, in packages marked 'battered onion rings'. We moved house yesterday. For many of us the chaos of moving home is temporary; a matter of inconvenience, while exchanging one form of security for another. For millions of people, though—asylum seekers, refugees, homeless families—dislocation is a fact of life. It is impossible to think of welcome, home and homelessness in the abstract. The homeless are not a category, but real people. Homes are shaped and brought to life by their occupants. Ordinary people guests and hosts—offer and receive hospitality.

Hospitality is a subject in itself, but we will also see the practice of welcome as a window onto wider issues of home and homelessness. Our story of hospitality (and inhospitality!) has a wider backdrop. This week, we begin with Old Testament hospitality before moving on, next week, to selected readings from the New Testament.

These notes use the New International Version.

8–14 OCTOBER

1 Under the trees of Mamre

Genesis 18:1–19

The familiar verse of Hebrews 13:2 urges hospitality to strangers, 'for by so doing some people have entertained angels without knowing it'. So Hebrews recalls Abraham, welcoming three special guests under the trees. As Abraham is described as 'father of the faithful' in Genesis 18, he appears as 'father of the hospitable'.

Much of Genesis 18 is, to use the internet jargon, 'off-topic'. We omit the messengers' promise of a son, Sarah's amused reaction (vv. 9–15) and Abraham's intercession (vv. 16–33), though this is relevant to tomorrow's account of Lot's rescue. Instead, here is Abraham, resting after dinner, seated by the shady entrance to his tent, in the heat of the day (v. 1). Then, suddenly, the Lord is encountered in a visitation of three strangers (vv. 1–2). Abraham's welcome shows a solicitous hurry (vv. 2, 6), but this is in stark contrast to the deadly haste of Genesis 19:1–29.

The visitors arrive at an inconvenient moment. Yet their appearance remains a great 'favour' (v. 3) and a 'providence' (v. 5b AV), while a lavish feast (vv. 7–8) is deprecatingly dismissed as a 'morsel of bread' (v. 5 RSV). Water is offered, to wash the dust of the journey off a guest's feet (v. 4). Abraham stands while his guests finish their meal (v. 8). All of these traits are mirrored in Bedouin practice, even to the present day.

For individualistic moderns, Abraham's predisposition to hospitality is an age away. Here is the nomad's world, where a reciprocal willingness to entertain the stranger could mean the difference between life or death, in a harsh desert climate. Later Jewish tradition notes that even in a culture where such behaviour was expected, Abraham was a generous man. Abraham, the story goes, kept an open doorway on each side of his tent so that any passing stranger would know that they were free to enter. The Mamre hospitality passage attracted even more speculative Jewish reflections from the tenth-century biblical commentator, Rashi. He identified the servant who prepared food for the three strangers as Ishmael. Thus, Rashi argues, Abraham taught his son the practice of welcome.

Not only Ishmael, but all the patriarch's descendants—by faith or kinship—find at 'Abraham's table' a baseline of hospitality and of expectation (Luke 16:19–31).

2 Rescuing citizen Lot

Genesis 19:1–14

By evening two angels arrived in Sodom (19:1), leaving Abraham interceding with God for his nephew and former companion, Lot (Genesis 18:16–33). They found Lot sitting in the gateway to this walled city (v. 1), appropriately for a respected citizen. Lot, separated from Abraham after an argument, first settling *near* Sodom (Genesis 13:10–13), then moved into the city (14:12). But Lot remembered hospitality. He opened his home, rather than leave strangers on the street (v. 2).

Traditionally, subsequent events feature an encircling mob, intent on raping Lot's guests while Lot offers his daughters instead. But, what was the crowd's intent (v. 5)? The word translated 'know' in older versions can mean 'to have sexual intercourse with', but only in a dozen of 936 occurrences. Usually, 'know' denotes simple acquaintance.

So, alternatively, the crowd suspect this newcomer, Lot, for taking in two strangers—potential spies—after dark. They gather to investigate (i.e. to 'know' them). When Lot offers his daughters (v. 8), he is not suggesting surrogate rapes, but providing hostages as a surety. The crowd included Lot's sons-in-law (vv. 12–14), whose families might have guaranteed their safety.

This interpretation is confirmed by Ezekiel 16:44–58, which identifies Sodom's sin. Sodom's inhabitants do 'detestable things' (Ezekiel 16:50)—a phrase mainly associated with pagan religious practices. They were also 'arrogant, overfed and unconcerned; they did not help the poor and needy' (Ezekiel 16:49–50). Thus, Sodom's sins were primarily social and religious.

This narrative asks the question, 'Who belongs'? Lot sits in the gate, like an insider (v. 1), but he is deluded. Abraham is, ironically, more at home in his tents than Lot is behind his walls. The populace regard Lot as an untrustworthy outsider (v. 9). Lot thinks he belongs, but fortifications and his coveted social status cannot substitute for the 'homefulness' of community, with God and with others. Sodom's pseudo-community is unstable.

Here, also, is a tale of hospitality and inhospitality. The flawed, righteous Lot welcomes strangers, although he is also a stranger. He defends the sacred hospitality of his house, even risking his own safety (v. 8). But the townsfolk abuse Lot's commitment to the stranger, overturning established expectations of welcome. As Ezekiel says, Sodom was an unfriendly place for travellers or marginal people. 'Sodomy' means inhospitality and soon, the inhospitable place became the uninhabitable place.

3 Heart of a stranger

Exodus 23:1–13

What is a stranger? A cluster of Hebrew words, variously translated, can mean outsiders, aliens, foreigners or sojourners (resident landless foreigners). For Israel—Abraham's heirs—differential access to the land created 'insiders' and 'outsiders'. Abundance did not guarantee equality. Sojourners were vulnerable, possessing neither land nor 'insider status', and so enjoyed God's special care, alongside widows, orphans and the poor.

What does it feel like to be a stranger? In today's reading from the so-called 'Covenant Code' (Exodus 20:22—23:33), Israel had a secret. They understood what it was to share 'the heart of a stranger' (v. 9 RSV)—their longings, insecurity and homelessness. Because Israel were sojourners, this experience should colour their attitude to strangers, inspiring a response of justice and open-hearted hospitality (v. 9).

A spirit of welcome, manifest in Abraham's example, came to inhabit the law which served Israel in more settled times. The covenant revealed a bias to the stranger, offering both command and motivation for action (v. 9). This predisposition went beyond simple hospitality. Inclusive welcome, not efficiency, should mark Israel's husbandry (vv. 10–11). God spread a table of abundance, from which strangers, marginal people and even 'wild animals' were able to share (v. 11). The sabbath is to be a hospitable space in which slaves, strangers and livestock may find refreshment (v. 12). God's hospitality, manifest in the open-handedness of God's people, embraced all creation, forming crucial elements of a social and ecological ethic. In this way, the ancient practice of reciprocal hospitality found a contemporary expression.

But surely—as towns replaced tents—settled times demand settled ethics? Not for Israel. The nomadic ethos and even the bitterness of bondage, wandering or exile, claimed a permanent place in Jewish cultural consciousness. Whether at home or away from home, God's people were still strangers and tenants and the land was still God's: 'The land must not be sold permanently, because the land is mine and you are but aliens and my tenants' (Leviticus 25:23). This principle applied alike for kings and commoners (cf. 1 Kings 21). The wilderness was always *now*, never a stage to leave behind, but an essential dimension of life in the land. Hospitality thus became an act of remembrance. To offer welcome is an experience of discovery, through the presence of a stranger.

4 Asylum seekers

Deuteronomy 23:1–7

'Q' entered Britain, from Zimbabwe, with her two children, 'L' and 'S'. She was assaulted (and worse) for distributing opposition leaflets. 'Q' now lives on vouchers and goodwill, while her son, 'S', suffered a racial attack. Their asylum application was refused, although they are appealing. 'Q' never received documents for this hearing. Reasons for refusal included 'non-attendance' at the previous hearing, *not* having a criminal record and failure to demonstrate a well-founded fear of persecution. Subsequently, their house in Zimbabwe has been burned and 'Q's brother murdered, in mistake for her. 'Q' speaks English and has a supportive church. Thousands more do not.

Yesterday we explored the position of Israel's 'resident aliens'. Deuteronomy continues this concern, acknowledging the stranger's precarious status (Deuteronomy 1:16; 10:18–19). Today's reading, however, reveals both the strengths and limitations of this tradition, asking the question 'Who may enter the assembly of the Lord (i.e. God's gathered people)?'

It is a troubling reflection on conflicts from Ireland to Palestine that memory can serve the cause of hatred. Offence, then and now, is remembered to the tenth generation (v. 3). Deuteronomy 23 envisages the inclusion, exclusion or conditional admission of foreigners depending on their historic treatment of Israel (vv. 3–8). Ammonite inhospitality (Numbers 22–24) provoked permanent exclusion from the assembly (v. 3) and a ban on treaties of friendship (v. 6). Yet Egyptians were treated favourably because Israel sojourned in their country (vv. 7–8). Remarkably, the Egyptian sojourn—for all its eventual oppression—was remembered as an act of Egyptian hospitality, which Israel felt obliged to reciprocate.

Such policies reflected ambiguities created by God's protection of marginal people on the one hand and the seductive political and religious influence of the surrounding nations, on the other. Amid Israel's nationalism a redemptive dimension sometimes seems lacking. A less conditional welcome awaited Jesus' table fellowship and the community of the early church, in which the alien became citizen. Here, the combination of a more outgoing ethos and the old 'stranger loving' made for a new, inclusive hospitality.

It is inadvisable to take the church's hospitality and turn it, simplistically, into political policy. Governments should be in no doubt, however, that Christian instincts towards asylum seekers and other 'sojourners' are shaped by a tradition which understands the 'heart of a stranger' and is committed to seek justice for vulnerable incomers.

5 A table in the desert

Psalm 23

If repetition made scripture banal, then Psalm 23 could be biblical muzak. But this poem's subtle power transcends such familiarity. Psalm 23 is sometimes called 'the shepherd psalm' but this is only partly accurate, since the metaphors shift from husbandry (vv. 1–4) to hospitality (vv. 5, 6). The maturity of the psalmist's knowledge of evil and suffering (vv. 4, 5) forms an undercurrent below apparently tranquil confidence.

Although this is an individual psalm, it echoes Israel's experience, especially of Sinai. The evocatively named 'valley of the shadow of death' (v. 4) mirrors Jeremiah's wilderness descriptions (Jeremiah 2:6). The desert is a place of pitfalls and darkness where no one lives or travels (Jeremiah 2:6). The desert is an inhospitable place, hostile to life and livelihood. The desert is the place of vulnerability, where there is only trust or death. Psalm 23, without sanitizing the desert's terror, highlights a qualitative difference between aimless wandering and purposeful journeying (vv. 1–4).

In Psalm 78:19 Israel wonders, 'Can God spread a table in the desert?', while God asks, 'Have I been a desert to Israel or a land of great darkness?' (Jeremiah 2:31a). In short, is God inhospitable? Psalm 23 addresses such misgivings. In inhospitable places (acutely exposing human frailty), God is hospitable. For travellers, separated from home comforts and security, there is welcome on the journey. The Lord offers the traditional elements of welcome (table, oil and cup) in abundance (v. 5). Oil (v. 5) was a customary courtesy for guests and not only for special occasions.

In closing, the psalm recalls pilgrimage and temple worship. There is an allusion to the thanksgiving offering (Leviticus 7:16; Deuteronomy 12:5–7; 1 Samuel 1:3–4, 9) and to a meal shared by God, worshippers and the priests. We are reminded of the limitations and the promise of hospitality. The guest is not 'at home' but dependent, temporarily, on another's generosity. Hospitality is not homecoming.

But eating together was more than a simple meal. It fostered relationships of mutual loyalty which could be the culminating token of a covenant (see Exodus 24:8–12; 1 Corinthians 11:25). We should be careful not to read into verse 6 later conceptions of eternity, but Christian perspectives do complement the psalmist's meaning. God's hospitality promises more than temporary respite. It anticipates a fuller 'homefulness', unlimited by time and circumstance (v. 6).

6 A feast for all peoples

Isaiah 25:1–9

Those of us who have organized weddings remember the awkwardness of getting the seating arrangements right. In cultures where eating together indicates acceptance, etiquette is even pricklier. Jesus' parable of the places at table (Luke 14:7–14) was not the first with a scandalous guest list. Isaiah pictures a banquet to which all peoples are invited, regardless of past enmities (v. 6).

Isaiah 25 offers two clusters of hospitality-related images of protection (v. 4) and abundance (vv. 6–8). The first deals with the security of God's people amid rapacious foreigners (vv. 1–5). The second is a joyous feast, with the finest food and a universal admissions policy. Verse 4 combines multiple images of God's protection—'shelter', 'refuge', 'shade'—perhaps more familiar in the Psalms. We should understand the 'poor' and 'needy' as God's downtrodden and apparently defenceless people.

In his *Praying the Psalms*, Walter Brueggemann notes a tension between two 'places': the 'pit' (also 'Sheol') and the 'wing' (also 'tent', 'rock', 'tower'). The former (often found in psalms of lament) represents the place of 'disorientation' or despair—the wrong place, where dignity is swept away and God appears absent. The latter is the place of 're-orientation', which enables the sufferer to challenge circumstances, renewed by fresh hope. This verse (v. 4) accentuates the protective aspects of hospitality. For the poor, God's hospitality is more secure than the fortified cities of their oppressors (v. 2). Indeed, hospitality can be seen as a sign of judgment on such false security.

Universalism is the belief that God's purposes were not limited to Israel but included other nations. Isaiah 25 is a fine example, though the chapter's conclusion reverts to a more conventional oracle against Moab (vv. 10–12). But, verses 6 to 9 are a pinnacle of hope. This banquet is open to all (Jews and Gentiles, v. 6). There is no 'top table', since the best is available to every guest (v. 6). Even 'all-consuming' death is itself swallowed up in celebration (v. 7).

This banquet is echoed in the New Testament, in Jesus' parables (Luke 14:15–24), apocalyptic expectation (Revelation 21:4) and above all in the Eucharist. Isaiah's vision foreshadows the coming of the hospitable kingdom, just as every act of hospitality anticipates a more perfect welcome, unbounded by hesitation or mortality.

Guidelines
Some highlights of this week's readings:
* In his hospitality, Abraham acts as a forerunner.
* Inhospitality is worthy of judgment.
* Concern for the stranger is built into Israel's consciousness.
* Old Testament commitment to welcome the stranger was conditional.
* Hospitality is limited by time and personal boundaries.
* Apparently frail hospitality contrasts with the false security of fortified cities. Yet, the tents of Abraham are safer than Sodom's walls.

- There are glimpses of a quality of welcome unbounded by time and reservations, to which every act of hospitality now points, as a sign.

1 Mission by numbers?

Luke 10:1–17

If you were responsible for a global mission, how would you proceed? Is it 'evangelism.com' and multimedia presentations? Once Luke's missionary mathematics are understood, it seems a symbolic 'worldwide mission' *is* what Jesus intended. It is no coincidence that the Greek version of the Old Testament (the Septuagint) lists 72 nations (Genesis 10). Jesus' approach is shocking. Worldwide mission begins with one person (Jesus) commissioning two people (two disciples) to share the message with some people (a household) and so reach more people (a town), before taking the gospel to all people (the world).

But this passage is not about clever numerology. Jesus' commission (vv. 1–4) is a mission to the house (vv. 5–7). Messengers should proceed purposefully and in haste (v. 4) with a trustful attitude, evident in travelling without customary resources of provision and protection (vv. 3–4). Provisions are unnecessary since the mission assumes a reciprocal exchange of service and hospitality, between messengers and hosts (vv. 5–9, 16). The preacher is to be welcomed as if the person sending the message were personally present (v. 16).

Moreover, the one welcoming the prophet shares in the prophet's reward, reaping the benefits of the kingdom of God—peace, teaching, healing and liberation (vv. 6, 9, 17; see Matthew 10:41). Luke 10 echoes 2 Kings 4:8–37. Hospitality is offered (2 Kings 4:8–10), and in return the Shunamite received the blessing of a son (2 Kings 4:17). Here also a messenger is sent instead of the prophet, in haste, with an urgent mission (2 Kings 4:29–31).

There are crucial clues to church growth in the mission of the 72.

The disciples should accept lodgings (v. 5), forming what, effectively, was a house church (v. 7). We should not view such households in terms of our own nuclear families. 'Household' in the first century was more holistic. It included the head of the house (usually male, though not always), family, slaves, servants and others, forming a hub for economic and religious practice. So, mission to the house targeted the foundations of Jewish and Greco-Roman society. Just as Jesus' 'on-the road' disciples relied on 'in-the-house' hospitality (Luke 8:3; 10:38–42), so New Testament churches maintained the hospitality/ service relationship between itinerant preachers and the household congregations: 'show hospitality to such men that we may work together for the truth' (3 John 8b).

2 Bethany

Luke 10:38–41

Sometimes centuries of interpretation encrust a passage like barnacles. Lot's rescue is one example and this story is another. Since Origen (c. AD185–255) mystical writers have made of Martha and Mary a parable of the 'active' and 'contemplative' life. So, Martha is the practical homemaker and Mary the reflective type. Usually, this tradition emphasizes the superiority of the contemplative over the active life, while acknowledging that 'Mary' and 'Martha' are needed in the church. Unsurprisingly, such interpretations have provoked some hostile feminist response.

Jesus was a frequent guest in Martha and Mary's home at Bethany, a village two miles from Jerusalem (Luke 10:38–42; John 11:1–53; 12:1–9). We know that Martha had taken the initiative in offering hospitality (v. 38). Luke's account is a call to discipleship, illustrating the high status Jesus accorded to women. Both women are portrayed in atypically responsible roles. Martha, not Lazarus, is the head of her household, taking the decision to 'open her home' (v. 38). Such responsibility was unusual for the time. Similarly, Jesus' defence of Mary (v. 42) should be seen as an affirmation of her rights as a disciple. For a woman to learn at a rabbi's feet violated tradition. We might surmise that Martha found the role reversal difficult.

The passage is partly about hospitality but more about the effect of Jesus' call to discipleship on gender roles. Hospitality, service or sitting at Jesus' feet may be an individual's calling but none are exclusively 'men's work' or 'women's work'.

When Jesus gently chides Martha, he highlights her distraction (v. 41). Service and hospitality are good, but neither practice exists for itself. Each is carried out for Christ's sake. A similar point is made in John 12:1–9 where Mary anoints Jesus with a jar of expensive perfume, scandalizing the assembled guests in the process. In John and in Luke, Mary has a keen sense of the point of the activity: 'only one thing is needed' (v. 42).

This story is not an example of the virtues of the contemplative over the active life, but rather an assertion that service or hospitality demand attention to the heart of the action and not only its efficient performance. Christ's rebuke to Martha did not include a call to Martha to 'give up hospitality and follow me', but it did re-establish the meaning of the occasion.

3 The great banquet

Luke 14:15–24

Jesus seems always to be eating. Sometimes he is host (Luke 9:10–17; sometimes he is guest (Luke 5:30; 7:36; 10:38; 14:1; 19:7). Appropriately, after the resurrection he was recognized in the breaking of bread (Luke 24:30, 31).

The parable of the great banquet occurs in the so-called 'Journey Narrative' (Luke 9:51—19:44). Previously we have noted a conjunction of the themes of journeying and hospitality. Similarly here, as Jesus encounters hospitality and inhospitality on the way to Jerusalem.

Imagine the scene: Jesus reclined at table in the house of a prominent Pharisee (v. 1). The atmosphere was confrontational (v. 1) and the after-dinner conversation matched the mood. Jesus told the parable of the places at table (Luke 14:7–14). Here, the Pharisees were criticized for regarding hospitality as a means to social advantage (vv. 12, 13) and challenged to consider a very different guest list

(v. 13). This gathering of scandalous guests is the thread which binds together both parables (vv. 13, 21–23).

In the days before refrigeration hosts relied on a two-stage invitation system. Initial notice was given some weeks beforehand. A second invitation was made at banqueting time. Hence the messenger's phrase 'all is now ready'. The amount of food required depended on the number of replies to the earlier invitation. If guests stayed away, mountains of food would be wasted. In the parable the invitees give weak, belated excuses (vv. 18–20), potentially humiliating the host. The owner responds by turning the tables, inviting anyone who will come in place of the first guests (vv. 21–23).

The new guests include Israel's outcasts (v. 21). The Qumran community anticipated that these people would be barred from the messianic banquet. Most commentators believe that the second group (v. 23) are Gentiles. So, the banquet of Isaiah 25 is partly fulfilled in Jesus' table fellowship. Yet, there is urgency. The meal will not keep and the time available to accept the invitation is limited. As with most good tales, there is a suspenseful ending.

Kenneth Bailey points out that by the conclusion of the parable, the guests have not yet assembled (vv. 23, 24; *Through Peasant Eyes*, p. 111). We are the guests of verse 23, unseen participants in a still unfulfilled parable. The story's completion awaits the coming of the hospitable kingdom when God's people will feast with Abraham, Isaac and Jacob (Luke 13:28, 29).

4 Discerning the body

1 Corinthians 11:17–34

The Eucharist went on a (prodigal's?) journey—from the house congregation to a church building and a real meal to a token celebration. When Paul writes, 'do this in remembrance of me' (v. 24), what did 'this' originally mean? As J.H. Yoder concludes, 'this' refers to an ordinary meal (*Body Politics*, pp. 14–16). Only later was the sacrament now called the Eucharist, the Mass, Holy Communion or the Lord's Supper, separated from everyday life: eating, drinking, social equality and hospitality. But in the rich language of this ordinance, a memory is preserved. 'Come, all is now ready' is both an invitation to the sacrament and a welcome to the lost world of Christian table fellowship.

Early Christians lived in a world as divided as ours. In Corinth Paul protested that status seeking had corrupted the life of the church. Perhaps the Corinthians were organizing the 'common' meal, in typical Greco-Roman fashion, with places of honour allotted according to social status (vv. 18,19). Even worse, poor people—slaves and artisans—worked long hours, often arriving late for the *agape* meal or 'love feast'. As a result, while the rich over-indulged themselves, the late comers went hungry (v. 21) and were humiliated (v. 22).

For Paul, 'one bread', 'one body' (1 Corinthians 10:17) is a way of affirming that the abolition of inequality in the church should be evident in the hospitality of the common table. When the Corinthians failed in 'discerning his body' (v. 29 RSV), they failed to recognize their poorer members as brothers and sisters in Christ. A meal which falls short of the demands of Christian hospitality, by excluding the poor, is not the Lord's Supper at all (v. 20), and inhospitality (as we have noted elsewhere) is liable to judgment (vv. 29–32). In our multinational economy, believers, rich and poor, sit around a global table. The relevance of Paul's words to the life of mainly affluent churches speaks for itself.

As the Eucharist says 'welcome', so every act of hospitality has a sacramental character. Jesus, present at the table, is welcomed in the stranger (Matthew 25:31–46). Both at the Lord's Supper and in hospitality, Christ is present in disguise. He is hidden under the ordinariness of the common meal and those who share in it, or encountered, unexpectedly, in the homeless person and the sojourner (Hebrews 13:2).

5 The ministry of hospitality

1 Peter 4:7–11

Addressed to 'God's elect, strangers in the world' (1 Peter 1:1), 1 Peter urges the sojourner's life for those who find hospitality in God's new household. As John Elliott indicates in his commentary on the epistle,

A Home for the Homeless, these 'strangers' are to be understood, literally, as a disenfranchised class of resident aliens. The addressees of 1 Peter were not Roman citizens and knew the outsider's frustrations. Not for the last time, Christianity offered dignity to the politically or socially marginalized.

In 1 Peter 4:9 a reference to hospitality occurs together with one of five lists of spiritual gifts (*charisma*) in the New Testament (Romans 12:6–8; 1 Corinthians 12:7–11; 12:28–30; Ephesians 4:11; 1 Peter 4:10). Their purpose is edification, building up the community of believers (1 Corinthians 14:26; 1 Thessalonians 5:11). Between brotherly love (in Greek, *philadelphia*, 1 Peter 1:22), hospitality (*philoxenia*, v. 9), service (*diakonia*, vv. 10–11) and 'household management' (*oikonomia*, v. 10), there is an intimate relationship. Where Christians were scattered, facing discrimination and hostility, a welcoming, well-ordered church was essential. Leaders had the duty to ensure edifying use of gifts and ministries in the congregation and encourage hospitality to vulnerable strangers (1 Timothy 3:2; Titus 1:8).

There is a difference—apparent to anyone on the receiving end—between a grudging and an ungrudging welcome. Offering hospitality 'without grumbling' (v. 9) is a gift (*charisma*), especially when guests are troublesome or arrive past midnight. Early Christians faced real difficulties. We know that refusing hospitality could be a matter of ecclesiastical politics (3 John).

Equally, not every stranger was an angel, for their hosts or the Christian community. In 2 John, the 'chosen lady and her children' (i.e. the church) are urged to deny hospitality to 'deceivers' (2 John 7–12). Peter was keenly aware of such people (2 Peter 2:1–22), but his insight is to avoid legislation in addressing the problem.

Although hospitality has boundaries (recognizing the dangers inherent in abuse of trust), those limits are established with an open attitude and an ungrudging spirit (v. 9). Such openness was courageous. The next guest might be an unreformed Saul. In Acts 9 we read how, three times, Christians accepted the risk of welcoming their former persecutor (Acts 9:17, 19, 26–30).

6 A tale of two leaders

The letters we know as 2 and 3 John address the matter of missionaries and the welcome they receive. Between the two epistles we have an insight into the challenges and limitations of hospitality. As the prophet's host shares the prophet's reward, so 2 John warns that those welcoming 'antichrists' (2 John 7) must share their judgment (2 John 11). 3 John, with its colourful cameos of leaders like Gaius (v. 1), Diotrophes (v. 9) and Demetrius (v. 12), balances the picture. John contrasts Gaius and Diotrophes, who serve, respectively, as examples of hospitality and inhospitality.

The addressee is Gaius (v. 1). We cannot be sure whether one of a number of men with an identical name (Acts 19:29; 20:4; Romans 16:23; 1 Corinthians 1:14) is the same person, but John identifies Gaius as his 'dear friend' (vv. 1, 2, 5, 11), known for warm hospitality (vv. 5–6). Gaius is encouraged to support missionaries with food and money (v. 6). So he followed Abraham (Genesis 18:16), whose welcome extended not only to sheltering strangers, but to providing for their ongoing journey.

Once again, Gaius illustrates the crucial relationship between itinerant and local ministry in early Christianity. Such provision was obviously a matter of debate in the churches, since a first-century manual called the Didache counsels, 'let the apostle receive nothing except bread, until he finds shelter' (*Didache* 11:8), and states, 'if he asks for money, he is a false prophet' (*Didache* 11:9).

By contrast, Diotrophes was a troublemaker (vv. 9–10), refusing hospitality to itinerant missionaries (v. 10) and breaking ties between John's circle and the church (v. 10). Diotrophes (from his name, probably an aristocratic Greek), was as inhospitable as Gaius was hospitable. Possibly he resented John's authority. Diotrophes regarded the church as a legitimate arena for petty politics, using inhospitality as a tool of social advancement.

Yet Diotrophes understood two things. First, he saw the link between hospitality and the guest's well-being. Hospitality provided room for mission and ministry to flourish. Second, he knew that hospitality was the glue which held together the ecumenical ties of the early church. In this way Diotrophes sought to hinder the missionaries and their task, while undermining John's authority. At heart, hospitality is the gift of space to a guest, friend or stranger. Within that space all manner of good things thrive: artistic achievement, mission, service, respite and healing.

Guidelines

Today, many aspects of biblical hospitality seem obscure or quaint. We find it hard to identify with the values of our nomadic precursors. But the tradition of welcome to strangers carries a wealth of meaning. Even the heartlands of Christian hope are described in terms of welcome (Isaiah 25:6–9; Luke 14:15–24).

Hospitality remains fertile ground for new experiments in Christian compassion. In the 1980s I worked for an organization in Leeds called Nightstop, which provided emergency accommodation for homeless young people in the homes of volunteer hosts. This initiative started with one person's practice of hospitality, the backing of two local churches and a willingness to be 'fools for Christ'. Today there are around thirty Nightstop projects. Hospices, shared church buildings, respite and foster care, Christian communities and work with asylum seekers all employ hospitality in creative new variations on an ancient practice.

However profound the significance of hospitality, it is the earthiness of these readings which comes across most clearly. They are about bread and water, practical economics, frosty welcomes, sweaty travellers, and the offer of space to strangers. In this ordinary, everyday way, guests and hosts are surprised and changed, to the incalculable benefit of the whole church. 'Do not forget to entertain strangers, for by so doing some people have entertained angels without knowing it' (Hebrews 13:2).

FURTHER READING

Kenneth E. Bailey, *Poet and Peasant* and *Through Peasant Eyes: A Literary-Cultural Approach to the Parables in Luke*, Eerdmans, 1983

Walter Brueggemann, *Praying the Psalms*, St Mary's Press, 1993

John H. Elliott, *A Home for the Homeless: A Sociological Exegesis of 1 Peter, Its Situation and Strategy*, SCM Press, 1982

John Howard Yoder, *Body Politics: Five Practices of the Christian Community Before the Watching World*, Discipleship Resources, 1992

EXODUS 25—40

The word 'exodus' means 'departure', and this is the name of the second book of the Old Testament. But the 'departure' that is spoken about in this book is a singularly important one—something much more significant than the hourly departure of the train to wherever. Rather, the 'departure' in the book of Exodus is akin to that 'departure' of Jesus that he himself spoke about, and which is recorded in Luke 9:31. That is, Jesus was 'departing' so that he could accomplish the work he had been sent to do, to bring about the deliverance of his people from their present restrictions.

That is the sense in which the word is used as the title of the second book in our Bibles. This book speaks of the 'departure' of the Israelite tribes under both the human leadership of Moses, and also, and no doubt even more so, under the divine guidance and leadership of the Lord. It will be a very long journey that ensues; the way will pass both through the sea and also across the desert, until eventually the people of Israel come to the promised land, and so to their new life. 'Free at last; free at last!' That is the real significance of their 'departure' from Egypt. It is the 'departure' that will set them on their way to wonderful new possibilities and great new vistas of life.

The earlier parts of the book of Exodus tell how the people of Israel came to be in Egypt (ch. 1), and about Moses and his call from God to save his people (chs. 2—4). Eventually the people go free (chs. 5—12), crossing the sea and giving thanks (chs. 13—15). Their travels (chs. 16—18) bring them to the mountain of Sinai (sometimes called Horeb in the Old Testament) where they are confronted with the greatness and glory of God, and receive his instructions for their ongoing life (chs. 19—24).

Then follow two blocks of material, and it is these that we shall be looking at this week and the next. These are chapters 25—31 which concern the making and the furnishing of the tabernacle, the desert sanctuary, those who would minister within it, and what would take place there; and chapters 32—34 which speak of Israel's sin in making the golden calf and Moses' prayers to God and his ministry on their behalf. There is much in these chapters about God's presence with his people, about their approach to him, about the call of God for his people's ongoing faithfulness despite grave human sinfulness, and about intercessory prayer.

The Bible version used for these notes is the New Revised Standard Version (NRSV).

Exodus 25:1—31:17

1 The tabernacle

Exodus 25:1–9

What is being spoken about here is a sort of portable church or chapel for the Israelites to use in their pilgrimage in the wilderness. We do not have to think that the Lord was expected physically to live in this place. The sense is, rather, that God's presence would surely be 'felt' by his worshippers in a particular way in that place, rather in the same way that we may feel the divine presence in a sacred building today. It is a matter that is given profound expression in a verse in Ezekiel, 'My dwelling-place shall be with them; and I will be their God, and they shall be my people' (37:27).

Some of the material used in the making of the tabernacle, such as animal skins and goat's hair (vv. 4f) may indeed have been readily available in the desert, and perhaps this desert sanctuary was akin to a nomad's tent, being constructed of skins draped on poles. But it would also seem that some other things spoken about here must reflect a much later age, one when the Israelite people were settled in the land of Canaan. It is not easy, for instance, to see how all the items mentioned in verses 6 and 7 would have been available in the desert!

The passage opens with the invitation to the Israelite worshippers to give of their own possessions for the building and decoration of the shrine. Not that they are under any sense of compulsion to do so, but rather are invited to give freely, yet at the same time generously. Such is surely the beginning point of the worship of God, a free response on our part to the God who himself has freely deployed his love and strength for us. Here in Exodus 25 is the response of the people to their God, the God who had heard their cry of distress in Egypt, and who acted lovingly and powerfully to save them.

Further, this sanctuary was intended to reflect something of the things of God. It was not to be made in any haphazard way, but in accordance with instructions that Moses received from God when he was on the mountain (that is on Sinai: 26:30). This is an indication of the fact that worship must come from God, his being and his ways, and always be directed towards him.

2 Table and lamp

Exodus 25:23–40

The very detailed instructions about the table and the lamp for the tabernacle may well seem to us to be a bit too much of a good thing, if not completely 'over the top'. But, of course, what is being written about here is believed by the writer to be of the greatest importance.

What is to be prepared to serve in the worship of God must be of the best, and must moreover be in accordance with what are perceived to be the instructions of God himself, given on the mountain to Moses (v. 40). That is, once again, there is to be nothing ill-considered or haphazard in this preparation for worship, or in the provision of furniture and artefacts for the sanctuary.

The liturgical purpose of the table (vv. 2–30) was to receive the non-animal offerings that were made to God. The principal offering would have been bread, in particular the Bread of the Presence (v. 30). This was intended to be a visible evidence of the presence of God with his people. No doubt at earlier times the thought was that here was something being offered for the deity to eat, but what is envisaged here is clearly a more spiritual conception of God than that. Here was the offering of one of the great staples of life being made to God.

The lampstand (vv. 31–40) was to be a symbol of God's presence, and thus was to be made of the most precious metal. What is being spoken about here is a seven-branched lampstand, whose purpose in purely practical terms was to give light in what would have been a dark sanctuary. Yet at a deeper level it was a highly visible representation of the presence of God, showing forth the light that the Lord gave for his people's pilgrimage, for so much of the time in dark places. That same God, in particular in his Son, is still the real source of our light (John 1:4; 8:12).

3 Altar

Exodus 27:1–8

Again, there are minute details and instructions given as to the construction of the altar for the desert sanctuary. In particular, there is to be an element of portability about this altar: it is to be equipped with carrying rods (vv. 6–7), for these worshippers are a pilgrim people. Moreover, whereas in ancient times most altars would have been made of stone, this one was of acacia wood, making it light. Alas, all too easily we build our sanctuaries in a massive way, so that they cease to have any mobility, and thus are we hindered as a pilgrim people.

It is not stated what the horns (v. 2) are for. Maybe they were to hold sacrificial animals in place while they were being sacrificed. We know from other parts of the Old Testament that they represented the protective presence of God, and provided some physical means whereby people could obtain refuge when their life was in danger (1 Kings 2:28–30). We have to say that it is not easy to understand the significance of the details about the 'grating' (vv. 4–5). Much clearer are the items detailed in verse 3: they are for attending to the sacrificial gifts—the shovel for ashes, basins for liquids, forks for animal offerings, special pans for the coals of fire. There must be nothing second-rate here; these utensils are to be made of bronze.

Upon this altar animal sacrifices would have been offered. The question may be asked how a wooden altar would stand up to such usage. It has been suggested that maybe it was filled with stones. Whatever in actual practice took place, the vision and the ideal here is of gifts being offered to the God who had already given new life to his worshippers.

4 Priests

We move on from the details of the sanctuary furniture to the people who will have particular religious responsibilities in the tabernacle. The whole of this long chapter is about the consecration of the priests, and no doubt there are ancient elements in this very detailed account. At the same time it would seem that there is much here that reflects the procedure for the consecration of the high priest and other priests in much later ages, perhaps even as late as the time after the Babylonian exile (587–539BC).

Perhaps all the details given here seem something of a rigmarole, but then we need to bear in mind that what is being dealt with here is a matter both solemn and significant. This is about nothing less than the setting apart of certain individuals who will work for the good of the people in the most holy place. These priests will be serving in what is believed to be the very near presence of the holy God. Their task will be to set in process ceremonies that will lead to the 'de-sinning' of the sinful people. They will be responsible for seeking divine forgiveness for the people. Therefore, in the first place it is vital that these priests are themselves cleansed from sin, so that they are prepared and fitted to serve their fellows. Thus will Aaron and his sons be 'consecrated' (v. 1: that is, 'set apart') for their holy duties.

Verses 1–3 speak of the animal and non-animal offerings presented to God on this occasion, in order to ensure the cleansing of those being consecrated. So also, Aaron and his sons are to wash (v. 4), and be made clean. They then receive particular items of clothing, sacral vestments that symbolize their office and holy responsibilities (vv. 5–6, 8–9), and finally they are anointed (v. 7). And thus these priests will be obligated forever in this service and ministry. That is, there are ministries instituted by God which are for as long as we are called by God to fulfil them—and not for some lesser time span that we may wish to choose. Finally—reverting to the desert sanctuary—the ceremony is sealed in the sacrifice (vv. 10–14) of the offerings mentioned at the beginning of the account (vv. 1–3).

5 Sacrifices and presence

Exodus 29:38–46

Although these verses have been tacked on to the account of the consecration ceremony of the priests, they are in fact about the regular daily sacrificial ritual. The passage is nearly equivalent to Numbers 28:3–8, and speaks of daily sacrifices both in the morning and in the evening. According to 2 Kings 16:15 the daily ritual was a burnt offering in the morning and a cereal offering in the evening, and that is probably what prevailed in the temple in Jerusalem in the time before the exile. What we have in Exodus 29:38–44—burnt offerings in both the morning and the evening—is most likely a reflection of what took place in the time after the exile.

What we are reading about here is what we might call daily morning and evening devotions, whatever form they take, whether they be corporate or individual, elaborate or simple, sacramental or non-sacramental. Here for the Israelites is their daily devotion to God, and the sacrifices are intended to be seen as a gracious provision of God whereby the relationship between God and people is maintained and developed. Nowhere does the Old Testament tell us what it is believed 'happens' when sacrifice takes place, but it would seem that we should understand that certain sins are forgiven, and that the worshippers are united in fellowship one with the other and with God.

And then all this is summed up in the closing verses of the chapter (vv. 45–46). These are truly thrilling verses for they speak of the promise of God that his presence will ever be with his people. There is, of course, no promise at all that God's people are going to be spared their own march through the wilderness, but they are assured of the divine presence with them, the promise with which Matthew's Gospel ends. Not only will the Lord be with them, but he will be their God, and they can be sure of that. The truth is that the Lord has committed himself in love to these people: 'I am the Lord their God' (v. 46).

6 Incense and sabbath

Exodus 30:34–38 and 31:12–17

What is special about the incense (30:34–38) is firstly the costliness of the ingredients that go into the making of it. But then, this is for nothing less than the worship of God, intended to be a pleasant smell whereby the Lord was believed to be a participant in the worship and the offering. And because this was for these divine purposes it must represent the best of what was available, and further must be prepared in the correct fashion. Hence all the very precise details given here. The 'stacte' was most likely some form of myrrh oil, the 'onycha' parts of a shellfish found in the Red Sea, 'galbanum' a resin, 'frankincense' a fragrant gum resin (v. 34).

Then what is special about this preparation of incense is that it is *only* to be employed in the worship of God, and not for any other purpose. That is, it is to be 'holy' to the Lord; it is to be separated out from normal uses associated with everyday life. It is to be wholly devoted to God. Certainly it must never be used by individual people for their own adornment (30:38). The warning is severe.

The matter of the sabbath (31:12–17), the seventh day of the week, our Saturday, has already been treated in Exodus 16:22–27 and 20:8–11, but here it is spoken about again. No doubt the institution of the sabbath goes back to very early times, but it came to have great significance and to assume a new importance in the times during and after the Babylonian exile (587–539BC). It was one of the distinguishing marks of the Israelite people. As is emphasized in this passage, this day is to be not only a day of rest for the people (modelled on God's day of rest), but it is also a particular sign of the covenant relationship between God and his people (31:16) and of the Lord's work of creation (31:17).

Guidelines

The background to the passages we have been studying this week has been the Israelites' desert wanderings. This is a harsh and demanding background indeed. And no doubt many today who turn to the scriptures feel themselves to be in desert ways and in wilderness terrain. This is not where we ourselves might have chosen to be.

Surely there are profound truths that come over the centuries to us today, truths about the worship of God, about the call to give of the best that we have to that worship, both of our goods and also of ourselves—whether we feel the call to be a part of a worshipping congregation or a particular call to leadership in worship and the work of the church. And there is assurance here for the days and the nights in the rough terrain, that we shall have the constant presence of God with us. As of old, so surely for all times. 'I am the Lord their God' (29:46). Thus:

> *By thine unerring Spirit led,*
> *We shall not in the desert stray;*
> *We shall not full direction need,*
> *Nor miss our providential way;*
> *As far from danger as from fear,*
> *While love, almighty love, is near.*

CHARLES WESLEY (1707–88)

Exodus 32:1—34:5

I The golden calf

Exodus 32:1–6

The previous week's readings were concerned with the divine provisions and regulations for the worship of God, and the maintenance of the Israelites' relationship with him. What we consider now is a series of passages that are concerned with the fact and the implications of a most serious endangering of that relationship. We read here of the people's great disobedience to God, what resulted from that, and what on their behalf Moses sought to do in order to ensure their continued life and the maintenance of the covenant relationship. Just at the time that the great act of disobedience takes place, Moses is absent from the people. In fact, he is up the mountain with God—and as a result of what he finds has happened among the people while he has been absent from them, he will return to that place with God.

The great sin of the people is, of course, the manufacture of a calf from gold (32:1–6). This was an attempt to fashion a god tangible and visible, a god who will do and say what the worshippers want him to do and say. But the Lord God is unique and he cannot be bent and manipulated to the wishes of his devotees—however tough may be their present lives. Nor will he tolerate any rivals: he calls for the total dedication of his worshippers, and will not share their worship with any other god.

Sadly, Aaron is deeply implicated in this drastic falling away from the worship of the Lord God alone. Perhaps the people felt that too much time was passing with Moses absent from them. What was he doing all this time up the mountain? They wanted some action! Indeed, their desire seems to have been for a god whom they could see was strong, one who would lead them on to the promised land. Thus the image they made was of a bull-calf. In Canaanite religious thought (and no doubt there is some reflection of that here) the bull was a significant religious symbol, representing both strength and fertility. Then to make matters worse, sacrifices were offered to this false god— and what looks suspiciously like an orgy took place (v. 6). Very probably we are intended to understand that this involved sexual immorality. What will happen now? In particular, what will happen to that divine and life-giving relationship between the true (and in fact the only) God and his people?

2 Intercession

Exodus 32:7–14

'What will happen now?' was the question with which the last section of notes ended. The answer is now given: Moses prays to God for his people. Interestingly, after all that we have been told in the preceding chapters in the book of Exodus about sacrifices for sins, there is no talk here of either sacrifices, or offerings, or incense. But then this is a matter far too grave to be dealt with by anything like that. This is a sin committed by what the Old Testament calls a 'high hand', and for that there is no sacrifice available to provide forgiveness (see Numbers 15:30–31).

Verses 7–10 speak of God's deep sense of anger over the sin of his people. This strong reaction of God may surprise us, but we can surely understand that the holy God cannot look upon sin without this sense of indignation. Human sin must inevitably give rise to divine displeasure and judgment. And thus there is the word of the Lord to Moses that Moses must leave God to himself and his wrath. Further, there is talk even of God destroying the people and of making a new nation of Moses: 'and of you [it is singular, Moses alone] I will make a great nation' (v. 10).

Thus it was that Moses implored God on behalf of his people. That is, Moses interceded for his sinful people, and it seems as if he used just about every argument he could think of to change God's mind: he would not want the Egyptians to gain the impression that God had acted badly (v. 12); Moses reminds God of his ancient promises to Abraham, Isaac and Jacob (otherwise known as Israel; see Genesis 12:1–3).

Amazingly—for verse 14 must be reckoned to be a very bold verse!—God does change his mind. We should not think that God is acting here in any easy or arbitrary way, but rather that he is responding to the importuning of Moses in mercy and compassion. It is this ministry of Moses that is remembered in Psalm 106:23, how Moses stood in the breach between his sinful people and God's righteous anger.

3 Further prayer

Exodus 32:30–35

We now have a further prayer by Moses on behalf of his sinful people. Although Moses is praying on the same subject as that of the prayer in verses 11–14, there is a definite new factor in this second prayer. Unfortunately, it is not entirely clear what the writer had in mind when he wrote of Moses saying to God, 'But now, if you will only forgive their sin—but if not blot me out of the book that you have written' (v. 32). We should think of the book being spoken about here as one that had the names of living people in it, a sort of 'register'.

But the question is, is Moses saying that if the people, sinful though they be, cannot be forgiven and continue in life, then he, Moses, wishes to have no further part in things? Is Moses making a strong affirmation to God that Moses and the Israelites are a 'unit', and that come what may, they are sticking together? Or, rather, is Moses saying that he is willing to give his life in order that his people may live? And if this is the thought here, then it is a fresh and original thought, one that is only taken up later in the passage about the suffering servant of the Lord in Isaiah 52:13—53:12, especially verse 5.

My own judgment is that it is this latter thought that is in the writer's mind. This would seem to be borne out by the wording of verse 30 with its, 'perhaps I can make atonement for your sin'.

But it must be said that things are left all rather vague at the end of the passage. There is talk about the Israelites moving on, and yet mention also of the coming judgment. Yet perhaps a certain vagueness is understandable, for who can fathom the mind of God, and who can speak more definitely about these ultimate matters, on the one hand, of the burning judgment of the holy God, and on the other, of his mercy and love for his people? At any rate, there seems to have been a plague, one that is interpreted here as being due to the judgment of God (v. 35).

4 The tent

Exodus 33:1–11

Now the people move on from the mountain and continue their march towards the promised land. They are promised the guidance of God, and—more—that he will go on ahead of them to drive out their enemies before them (v. 2). This may sound harsh, rather nationalistic to us, but we should perhaps seek to understand it as expressing a sense of God's protective and enabling presence with his people. This is God preparing the way before them, making it smooth, removing the barriers.

But at least the people seem somewhat chastened, mourning their sins, and putting aside their ornaments (v. 4). The last time we heard of their ornaments was when they were being offered to Aaron so that the calf of gold could be made (32:24). At least this removal of ornaments is a sign of repentance.

Verses 7–11 go on to deal with another subject, namely the desert 'tent of meeting'. Whether this tent was originally the same as the tabernacle (Exodus 25–27), or whether they were different, we really do not know. Certainly, in the account that we have here of the tent it is a much simpler, less elaborate structure than the tabernacle. This tent is the place where God and Moses meet. The passage does not actually say that Moses prayed to God there, but the language is certainly about the conversation between friends, God and Moses. It is at the same time marvellous, moving and encouraging. We may perhaps only understand the full wonder of this by reading Exodus 33:20 with its talk about no one being able to see God and live.

But then, this is the wonder of the personal relationship that the holy and totally 'other' God has with individuals of the frail and sinful people of earth. It is only when we understand what is being expressed in the thought of Exodus 33:20 that we can appreciate the wonder of the life of faith, and the privilege we are offered in this friendship with God. But in that desert tent, 'the Lord used to speak to Moses face to face, as one speaks to a friend' (33:11). And that privilege is surely still offered.

5 God's presence and his glory

Exodus 33:12–23

Moses had on an earlier occasion tried to prise some details out of God, something in particular about who God is, and what is his name (Exodus 3:13–15). Now at this later stage Moses seeks further clarification: Who will help him in this daunting task that God has given him (v. 12), and how does God wish to be served by Moses (v. 13)? We should understand that for Moses these are questions that urgently need answering. And it is not from any purely selfish motives that Moses asks this. It is rather that he is forced to a new reliance upon God, and all that God can offer him, because of the sheer magnitude of the task.

Yet Moses is not given any detailed response to his request. He does, however, receive a great promise, namely that God's presence will go with him (v. 14). Moses will still have to carry the great burden, and no doubt the unspoken thought here is that he will have to make many decisions on the way. But he is assured of this presence of God with him, and thus his mind should be at rest, his anxiety should be dispelled. In the midst of the challenge of his calling to the divine service there is also this secondary promise, 'I will give you rest' (v. 14).

Yet the matter is not over, for there is a further promise. It is that God will know Moses by name (v. 17). It was not given to Moses to know the name of God (Exodus 3:13–14), but God did know Moses' name. For this covenant relationship between God and his people was in no way a relationship of equals. God was the Lord, and Moses was his servant. Still, we can only stand amazed at the privilege for Moses, and for us all, when God says, 'I know you by name.'

Even so, Moses is not permitted to see God, only to be promised the merest glimpse. And yet that should be sufficient (vv. 18–23), as indeed we are told that to touch Jesus' garment was sufficient for his healing power to be felt in a sick woman's life (Mark 5:28).

6 Moses' face

Exodus 34:29–35

This subject here seems rather out of context with the passages we have been reading. It comes in connection with the renewal of the covenant relationship between God and his people, with Moses receiving the new tablets of the law (Exodus 34:1–28). Now we read of Moses coming down from the mountain with his face shining (v. 29). This was because he had been speaking with the Lord. Thereby something had happened to him, no doubt inwardly, but something so powerful that it had affected him outwardly. The text seems to be saying that Moses' face glowed with a supernatural light.

We may notice, incidentally, that the Hebrew word for 'shine' is similar in sound to the word for 'horn', and thus Jerome's Latin translation of the Bible (the Vulgate) has Moses being 'horned', with the curious result that the famous sculpture of Moses by Michelangelo has him complete with horns. But it seems clear from the context that 'shine' is the word intended—not 'horns'!

And such was the brightness of Moses' face that he put a veil over it so that the people were not so uncomfortably dazzled (vv. 33–35). But it made clear the fact that Moses and his people were back in favour with God, that they were not to be henceforth in darkness—for so much was suffused with light.

But this shining of Moses' face also speaks of the reflected glory of God. The one who has been in the near presence of God has caught something of the divine nature, and that is now being reflected on to others. As indeed we have known saintly ones who have reflected something of the divine light and life of God into our lives. And that has surely been because they have lived in close fellowship with God.

Guidelines

Our readings this week have taken us into two worlds, those of earth and heaven. The setting of these Exodus passages has been that of the seeming slow progress of the Israelites through the difficulties and harshness of the desert. Sin indeed has abounded. And yet on the mountain Moses has sought the presence of God, and has received the promise that that presence will continue. So also will Moses find rest from his worries.

And how remarkably has Moses been portrayed, this man who is at home both in the desert and on the mountain. He is the man who both works in the world, and is also to be found in prayer on the mountain, the man who is both with his people and also in fellowship with God. He is moreover the man who in a moment of deep crisis for his people boldly interceded on their behalf to God, and who seeks new life for the doomed sinners. He also, it would appear, is the one who offers to give his life that others may live.

There is surely much here for our onward pilgrimage through life. Here on the one hand is the promise of the presence of God with us in spite of our sinfulness, and yet here is the challenging call to both servanthood and saintliness. For who is there today who will intercede on behalf of the sinful people of earth, and who is there willing—if this is what is required—to give their lives that others may live?

FURTHER READING

R.E. Clements, *Exodus*, Cambridge Bible Commentary Series, 1972
(Unfortunately out of print now, but worthwhile if you can find a second-hand copy)

R.J. Coggins, *Exodus*, Epworth Commentary Series, 2000

M.E.W. Thompson, *I Have Heard Your Prayer: The Old Testament and Prayer*, Epworth 1996

MARK 6—10

The theme of the first set of readings in Mark's Gospel was Beginnings. We saw how the coming of Jesus introduced a new beginning into the relationship between God, Israel and the world. It was a new beginning for the people who left everything to follow Jesus around Galilee, and for individuals and groups on the margins of Israel.

Mark's Gospel is a narrative of revelation. God discloses his purposes for Israel and the world in the events that take place around Jesus. And the response Jesus looks for is faith. Though he makes little headway with those closest to him, and excites opposition from those who find his cause threatening, some show great faith in approaching him for healing and to hear his teaching.

Faith is the theme of the next four weeks' readings. We shall see the disciples continuing to struggle with their faith. But the faith of Jesus shines through, as the summons to enter God's kingdom and the inspiration to live in the way of the Messiah.

The readings are based on the Revised English Bible (REB), though they can be used with any modern version of the Bible.

Mark 6:1—7:13

1 Honouring faith

Mark 6:1–6

Jesus is from Nazareth (1:9, 24), but in 2:1 Capernaum seems to be his home town. People there have already recognized the authority of his teaching, and his power to heal and declare God's forgiveness. This time their amazement carries a note of incredulity. 'The fear of the Lord is the foundation of knowledge' (Proverbs 1:7). If Jesus' wisdom is not divine, as the questions in verse 2 suggest, then perhaps it is demonic, like his power to drive out demons (3:22). The townspeople allow what they know about Jesus' occupation and family to pass judgment on him: a carpenter cannot possibly be a prophet. And Jesus' remarks in verse 4 hint that his family are willing to collude with local opinion.

Why is there such a dim view of Jesus in Capernaum? Why are the people there so unwilling to recognize the source of his authority and honour his faith? Mark's readers know that Jesus is not bound by blood and soil. He is God's beloved Son, anointed by the Spirit, the messianic agent of God's redeeming rule, the divine mouthpiece who stands at the leading edge of God's new world. In the end, the locals' attitude boils down to a lack of faith. Jesus has, of course, been struggling to encourage his disciples to honour him with their faith. And faith has come from surprising quarters, notably marginalized and powerless people like the bleeding woman in the previous chapter. But in Capernaum there is a 'want of faith' (v. 6) which only astonishes Jesus.

The consequences of unbelief are serious. 'He was unable to do any miracle there' suggests that the kingdom of God is all but stopped in its tracks. Matthew softens any hint of Jesus' powerlessness ('he did not do many mighty works there'—Matthew 13:58), but Mark's impression is of a piece with the world created by the parable of the sower (4:3–9). Capernaum is like the path that gives no opportunity for the seed to take root. The kingdom of God relies on faith, not coercion. Those who do God's redeeming work must always reckon with the risk of rejection, even from those who claim to know them best.

2 Missionary faith

Mark 6:7–13

At last the Twelve are given something to do! In 3:14, Jesus called them to be with him and to act with his authority. So far they have learnt by observation, listening, questioning, reflecting, as Jesus has demonstrated the power and scope of God's kingdom. Now is the time for them to learn by doing—sharing Jesus' work by exercising his faith.

They are 'sent out' as apostles (see 6:30; the Greek for 'send' is *apostello*). Going 'two by two' will provide protection (like the stick to ward off wild animals) and support, and also strengthen their testimony to God's kingdom (Jewish law required the evidence of two witnesses). To 'take nothing' but the bare essentials means that they will have to live by faith, relying on the hospitality and generosity of others. Like Jesus, they cannot take a welcome for granted, and where they are rejected they must learn to leave their detractors behind. Shaking the dust off their feet is a vivid illustration of the serious consequences of unbelief, which can play no part in the work of God's kingdom.

There is the barest outline of the apostolic message and activity. The work of the Twelve is directed towards the marginalized (the sick and the demonized), implicitly in the name of God's kingdom, which people are called to embrace by repenting. Notice that there is no mention of gathering converts, only of extending the work of Jesus, whose own ministry acts as a model for missionary faith.

How far can today's followers of Jesus imitate these first apostles of God's reign? The settings of Christian mission may be entirely different from the towns and villages of Galilee. Assumptions about hospitality and support vary from place to place. But those who are called to extend the work of Jesus, in whatever way, must learn to live by the same missionary spirit: the *faith* that honours the way of Jesus above all things, a willingness to *travel lightly*, a conviction about the *importance* of the work of the kingdom, a desire to press home the *challenge* of God's reign, and the determination to include the *marginalized* in the order God wants to create in the world. How far does the church give the impression that it lives by this missionary faith?

3 Martyr faith

Mark 6:14–29

Mark tells us of the range of people who are interested in Jesus: from peasants and artisans to members of the religious élite, and now a powerful political ruler. The Herod here is Antipas, one of the sons of

Herod the Great (the Herod in the Christmas stories). He governed Galilee and Perea (the region to the north east of the Dead Sea) from 4BC to AD39 with the permission of the Romans, who often ran their empire through local rulers.

Throughout the Gospel, questions have been asked about Jesus and the source of his authority. Here we have some indication of public opinion. Jesus is compared to the prophets, particularly Elijah, whom many believed would return to prepare Israel for the coming of God's kingdom. Jesus is even being mentioned in the same breath as the local hero, John the Baptist. More than that, claim some: Jesus is 'John the Baptist... raised from the dead'.

Though we have known since 1:14 of John's arrest, only now in this narrative flashback are we told how he died. The Herodian family tree was complicated, and riddled with incestuous relationships. According to the Jewish historian Josephus, Herodias was Herod's half-niece, and was formerly married to his half-brother Philip. John's criticism of high-level corruption is hardly surprising. Herodias took exception, persuaded her husband to have him arrested, and seized her opportunity to get rid of him. However much sympathy Herod had for John, it was no match for his desire to save face after the rash promise he made at his birthday banquet.

John the Baptist falls victim to the intoxications of power. The hallmark of his martyr faith is his determined defence of the law of Moses, and his courage to say what is unpalatable to one who holds the power of life and death. His martyrdom paves the way for the mightier one (1:7). Whoever Jesus might be (and we have not yet had an explicit answer to the questions swimming around in Mark's story), he too has martyr faith in common with his forerunner.

4 Nourishing faith

Mark 6:30–44

With the return of the Twelve, Jesus hopes to reflect with them on their preaching and healing. That way he will nourish the faith that has often been slow to see the significance of his own ministry. But the expectations surrounding them are such that privacy is impossible.

The crowds, drawn from nearby towns and villages, are hungry for his teaching and inspiration. Rather than look for a way of escape, Jesus can only meet them with compassion. He sees them as 'sheep without a shepherd' (v. 34), something that Moses had never wanted Israel to be (Numbers 21:17). They are like their ancestors who were neglected by greedy and oppressive rulers, left as it were to wander over mountains as prey for wild animals (Ezekiel 34:5–6).

What is the significance of Jesus' feeding this crowd? It is worth noting the contrasting responses of Jesus and the disciples. Not unreasonably, they see the solution in terms of buying bread. But Jesus expects them to use their faith and imagination to draw on all the resources available to them, material (however meagre the five loaves and two fish may appear) and spiritual. If they have seen the power of Jesus operating through the natural order, can they not trust him to feed a crowd as Elisha did with only twenty loaves (2 Kings 4:42–44)? After all, people are saying that Jesus is 'a prophet like one of the prophets of old' (6:15).

The feeding shows that Jesus is more than a prophet. Ezekiel had hoped that one day God himself would come as a messianic shepherd, another King David, who would search for his sheep, tend the wounded, strengthen the weak, and feed them with justice (Ezekiel 34:11–16). So the feeding of the five thousand is an image of liberation: God comes to redeem his people from greed and oppression through his shepherd Jesus. How then will Jesus nourish them? Perhaps the crowd see themselves as a potential army of liberation— 'companies of fifty and a hundred' (v. 40) may have military overtones —ready to follow Jesus, their new David.

But Jesus will not fight greed and oppression through violence. His fourfold action (taking the food, blessing God for it, breaking the loaves and giving them to the disciples—v. 41) anticipates his last meal with the disciples, so that his gift of abundant bread symbolizes the power of his ultimate sacrifice. Jesus will establish God's kingdom by giving his life, not by taking life from others. His faith will nourish Israel with justice, but like John the Baptist, it will cost him dear.

5 Astounding faith

To understand the sequel to the feeding of the crowd, we need to spot the connections with the exodus story. Notice how Psalm 78:13–25 links the passage through the Red Sea and the feeding in the wilderness. Here the disciples make heavy weather of their sea crossing. Jesus walks across the sea, though not to rescue them. They are in no danger, and he intends to pass them by. Leaving aside the issue of whether or not Jesus could have walked on water (the idea that he was walking in the shallows is discounted by the fact that the disciples' boat is in the middle of the lake), Mark makes it clear that he is not merely the successor of Moses, but a greater figure—feeding God's people with bread, and walking over the sea.

There are other links with the exodus story. Like Moses, Jesus climbs a mountain to pray (v. 46), and when he comes down the people are astonished (see Exodus 34). The wind on the lake blows from the direction of Bethsaida (north-east); in Exodus 14:21 a strong east wind, blowing all night, parts the Red Sea. And just as God reveals his name to Moses, so Jesus identifies himself to the disciples with words that translate the divine name: 'it is I' in verse 50 renders the Greek *ego eimi*, the 'I am' of Exodus 3:14.

As in the earlier story of the stilling of the storm (4:35–41), Mark is once again answering the question his narrative keeps raising: 'Who is this?' The disciples make heavy weather of everything that is being revealed to them. They do not understand what the feeding means, so they cannot make the connections between Jesus, Moses, the prophets and the messianic hope. As if to press home his message that the day of Israel's redemption has dawned, Mark once again highlights Jesus' healing ministry—something that the prophets associated with the messianic age (see Isaiah 35). But these astounded disciples miss the point. Whatever faith they may have, it has not been nourished by the feeding or strengthened by the incident on the lake. Their closed minds bring them perilously close to those Pharisees who stand in Jesus' way (3:5).

6 Consecrating faith

Mark 7:1–13

The Pharisees were a Jewish renewal movement who wanted to extend the priestly laws to the whole of life as a way of consecrating Israel to God. The scribes—some of whom were Pharisees—were theologians, interpreters of the law who applied its meaning to the circumstances of everyday life. Both groups were concerned with holiness, loyalty to God, faithfulness to the law of Moses.

At the time of Jesus, Jewish territory was part of the Roman empire and Jewish life was strongly influenced by Greco-Roman culture. Scholars sometimes refer to this as a 'double occupation'. It shaped the Pharisees' and scribes' understanding of holiness. To be holy, faithful Jews must maintain their distinctive identity, and to a certain extent keep themselves separate from Gentiles, and even from Jews who were unconcerned about loyalty to their ancestral people.

This kind of consecrating faith showed itself in social life and religious practice. Pharisees would avoid certain kinds of people, and set great store by actions that set them apart from others—such as the ritual cleansing referred to in verses 2–4, and the tradition of 'corban' in verses 11–12. As we have seen, Jesus and his group shared none of these scruples. They believed in holiness, but theirs was a different kind of consecrating faith, one that sought to find ways of renewal for all Israel—'insiders' as well as 'outsiders'—as God's covenant people.

Not all Pharisees would come under the condemnation found in verses 6–8, only those who strongly opposed Jesus' more inclusive vision of God's kingdom. The tradition of 'corban' is a good example of what we might call a more sectarian approach to the law. Moses regarded relationships with parents as sacrosanct, but some would rather give, or at least promise, money to the temple than support them. This is an example of the self-serving holiness that Jesus can only see as hypocrisy. The Pharisees and scribes would doubtless defend themselves by claiming that they were in fact teaching the way of God's commandments, but Jesus accuses them of peddling human teachings. They are merely promoting the interests of élite groups like their own, at the expense of those they write off as having no hope of sharing in the coming age of salvation.

If faith is to consecrate the world, it must somehow find room for those who don't fit into its vision of holiness. Try to find some contemporary examples of the sectarian approach within and beyond religion. What do you think Jesus would have to say to these?

Guidelines

Looking back over this week's readings, we can see some of the different dimensions of Christian faith.

- Faith does not simply believe in the existence of Jesus, but honours him as the one who speaks and acts for God.
- Faith is prepared to play its part in the work of God's kingdom, even at the risk of misunderstanding and rejection.
- Faith does not rely on its own resources, but is nourished by Jesus himself, even when it is completely mystified by him.
- Faith looks beyond its own religious community and offers itself as a resource for renewing the wider world.

How much do these dimensions of faith inform your faith?

Mark 7:14—8:26

1 Heartfelt faith

Mark 7:14–23

Jesus shifts his attention from washing to food. Both are concerned with the body. Washing takes place on the surface of the body, food crosses the boundary between the body and the wider world. Anthropologists point out that the body can be seen as a symbol of society. What takes place at the extremities (washing, clothing, contact with others) and what is allowed in and out (food, bodily excretions) symbolize relations between a community or culture and the wider world. Insights like these help us understand the significance of Jesus' teaching here and elsewhere in the Gospel about what are often called 'purity' issues—eating, touching, socializing, washing.

In verse 6, Jesus criticized the Pharisees and scribes for their hypocrisy. The Greek word *hupokrite* means 'mask'. Actors in the theatre often wore these masks. They were 'hypocrites' in the sense that there was something else behind the image they presented to their audiences. Jesus accuses his detractors of hiding their hearts—their true selves, where the thoughts and attitudes that find expression in behaviour lie—behind their teaching and practices.

Jesus insists that rules about food are far less important than what lies behind them. For these Pharisees and scribes, what happens at the boundaries of the body (washing, eating) shows how they see themselves and their community in relation to the wider world. If they imagine that they are somehow defiled by contact with those they regard as 'outsiders', it is because they view such people as unclean in themselves: unworthy of belonging to God's people because they are 'not like us'. Attitudes like these inform all kinds of sectarianism, and are the basis of violence and social disorder (notice how the 'evil things' Jesus mentions in verses 21–22 destroy community life and fuel chaos). By looking behind the mask to the heart, Jesus exposes the thoughts and values that set individuals and communities at odds with one another.

Mark's aside at the end of verse 19—'by saying this he declared all foods clean'—was important in the multiracial church for which he was writing. It reinforces Jesus' teaching that we are not defiled by what happens at the boundaries of the body, but by what lies within us. We must be careful, however, not to use these insights to diminish the contribution of social and economic factors to the human condition. It is surely right to look for the wider causes of crime, illness, underachievement and the rest. What is important, though, is to take seriously the impact of these on 'the heart', so that we can understand the way that wider influences make us what we are.

2 Educating faith

Jesus travels 30 miles north-west to the coastal region, Gentile territory. He is still searching for the seclusion that has eluded him since the Twelve returned in 6:30. We have met a parent coming to him on behalf of a daughter earlier in the Gospel (Jairus, a high-ranking Jew and president of the synagogue, in 5:22). But the one who violates Jesus' privacy here could hardly be more different. To respectable Jews she is triply disadvantaged: a woman, a Gentile, defiled by contact with her 'unclean' daughter. What she does in coming to Jesus is unusual: women do not seek men out in this way. But convention has to stand aside for desperation.

Jesus speaks as a Jewish male, though it is not clear why he responds as he does. The fact that she has to beg him to help her daughter may mean that he resents her intrusion, although he makes no attempt to drive her away. If 'the children' he is feeding first are the Jews, is he telling her that he does not see Gentiles like her and her daughter as a priority? Is he insulting her by using a typical Jewish term of abuse for Gentiles—'dogs'? And if Jesus is being difficult, why is this? Is he wanting to put her off, or to find out what lies in her heart?

She is not the first Gentile Jesus has met in this Gospel: he healed the seriously demonized Legion in 5:1–20. It is worth noting that Jesus is prepared to engage with this unknown, intrusive, Gentile woman. 'Let the children *first* be fed' may be designed to give her hope: her daughter's turn *will* come. The exchange about dogs is significant. In Jewish towns and villages they roamed the streets in packs, searching for food. They were regarded as dirty and a nuisance. The woman's reply suggests that in her culture, dogs were household animals, who were fed on scraps from the family table (if Jews fed the dogs that ran around outside, they would need to 'throw' bread to them, as Jesus indicates).

Perhaps the woman plays Jesus' saying about feeding dogs back to him as a way of revealing what lies in her heart—nothing less than faith. In her eyes, she and her daughter are not nuisances on the outside of Israel, but members of God's household. Her faith educates

Jesus—draws out the response she hopes for from him, and enables him to cross the boundary between Jews and Gentiles, men and women, clean and unclean. She helps to reveal a Jew in search of seclusion as the Messiah for yet another set of outcasts.

3 Releasing faith

Mark 7:31–37

This is hardly the most direct route back to Galilee—Sidon is 20 miles north of Tyre along the coast—but it gives Jesus the chance to remain in Gentile territory. Whether or not the man brought to him is a Gentile, Mark does not say. Notice how Jesus acts:

- First, he deals with the man privately. Unlike some popular healers and magicians, Jesus takes him to one side, away from the public gaze. He is not to be treated as a side-show, or a publicity stunt for a jobbing healer.
- Second, he treats him respectfully. By touching the man's ears and his tongue, Jesus establishes communication with him, using a form of 'sign language' to show him what he was about to do.
- Third, Jesus acts faithfully. By looking up to heaven—as he did before he fed the five thousand (6:41)—he acknowledges the source of his healing power. His ability to heal does not rely on technique but his faith, which allows him to act as a channel for the mercy of God.
- Fourth, he heals the man without any fuss, uttering a single Aramaic word—*Ephphatha*—which has been preserved in the tradition (cf. *talitha cum*, his words to Jairus' daughter, in 5:41).

Jesus' healing ministry was not unique, but the way he healed was of a piece with the compassion and respect he showed towards others generally.

Jesus' request for secrecy after a healing is something we have got used to by now, as is the difficulty people have in complying. But there is more to their publicizing here than mere gossip. 'He makes the deaf hear and the dumb speak' echoes those scriptures that look forward to the day of salvation. For example:

> *Then the eyes of the blind will be opened,*
> *and the ears of the deaf unstopped.*
> *Then the lame will leap like deer,*
> *and the dumb shout aloud;*
> *for water will spring up in the wilderness*
> *and torrents flow in the desert. (Isaiah 35:5–6)*

Salvation releases a man's ears and tongue, and reaches into Gentile parts. As faith extends, the walls around holiness are falling.

4 Extending faith

Mark 8:1–10

It is possible that this second feeding of a great crowd is a Gentile equivalent of the earlier feeding of the five thousand. Apart from the numbers involved, the two stories are almost identical. Mark may wish to suggest that Jesus is still in Gentile territory. *Four thousand* may be a hint at the four corners of the world, and *seven* the seventy Gentile nations. But this could be far-fetched.

The reason for the repetition may lie in the disciples' question in verse 4. After all they have seen, how can they possibly be so lacking in faith and imagination? What a contrast between these privileged, male insiders and the equally disadvantaged Syrophoenician woman! Perhaps Mark uses this incident as a way of heightening the tension in his narrative, as it moves towards Peter's confession and Jesus' declaration of the essence of his messiahship in 8:27–30.

One of the similarities in the two feeding stories is found in the words that convey Jesus' motivation. What Mark infers in 6:34 is here made explicit in verse 2: 'my heart goes out to them'. Between 6:34 and 8:2, there has been a lot about human hearts. What lies in the heart of Jesus is the best guide to the kind of holiness he looks for. His thoughts and attitudes allow him to reach out to those in real need, and translate holiness into practical action. And if it is that the four thousand he feeds here are largely Gentiles (verse 3 suggests that some have travelled a long way, and so could well be Jews), we have an example of a practical holiness that responds to human need irrespective of social, cultural or sectarian divides. When Jesus provides an abundance of 'bread in this remote place' (v. 4; the Greek word is *eremos*, often translated as 'desert'), he is like a greater Moses feeding an extended Israel, making it clear that there are no hard and fast boundaries around the covenant people of God.

5 Faith not signs

Earlier in the Gospel, Jesus had provided his critics with a sign of his authority to declare God's forgiveness to the paralysed man: 'Stand up, take your bed and go home' (2:11). But this time, 'no sign shall be given to this generation'. When they report this saying, Matthew (12:38–39 and 16:1–4) and Luke (11:29) have Jesus make an exception, in 'the sign of Jonah'. In Matthew 12 this hints at the death and resurrection of Jesus, and elsewhere refers to the repentance of the Ninevites. Perhaps Mark has 'no sign' because he wants to insist that faith has to do without the kind of evidence that would put the authority of Jesus beyond all reasonable doubt.

The disciples' struggle to believe and trust in Jesus shows that faith has to live with the angularities of his person and ministry. He fits, but at the same time does not fit. He fulfils ancient and popular hopes and expectations, but goes beyond (and sometimes contrary to) the prophets and their interpreters. He is as insistent as the most zealous Jew about the need for holiness, but his is of a totally different kind—though he roots it in the teachings of the scriptures. Little wonder the disciples, and others in the Gospel, struggle to make sense of Jesus.

Bread has hardly been out of the story since the feeding of the five thousand. Here once again Jesus uses it as a metaphor, but his appeal to imagination is lost on the disciples. When he speaks of 'the leaven of the Pharisees and of Herod', they can only think about the bread they've forgotten to bring. In the light of 3:6 and 6:16, 'leaven' refers to the corrupting influence of violence. 'Bread' signifies the power of Jesus to overcome the violence that divides one from another, and feed both Jews and Gentiles with justice. That way he starts to create a new and inclusive world of abundance and life. But for all their privileges, the disciples have defective 'eyes' and 'ears', minds and memories. They cannot work out the meaning of what they hear and see taking shape around them. Their only success, it seems, lies in exasperating Jesus.

For all this, the Twelve are role models of a kind. If those disciples who were closest to Jesus during his ministry struggled to understand him, those who are forced to live at a distance (the vast majority) should not expect faith and trust to come easily. Jesus never quite fits; faith never gets the measure of its object. In the absence of incontrovertible signs, faith is always striving to believe and trust.

6 Signs of faith

Mark 8:22–26

You may find it helpful to read 7:31–37 again, alongside today's passage, which is only found in Mark. The similarities with the earlier story are striking:

- Verse 22 (cf. 7:32): people bring along a sick man and beg Jesus to touch him.
- Verse 23a (cf. 7:33a): Jesus deals with the man privately.
- Verse 23b (cf. 7:33b): Jesus uses 'sign language' to communicate his intentions.
- Verse 26 (cf. 7:36): Jesus wants to avoid publicity.

There is, however, a notable difference. This time the healing is not instantaneous. At first the man's sight is only partially restored: people 'look like trees... walking about'. We might want to say that at this stage he can only see shapes. He has to wait for Jesus to lay hands on him a second time before he can 'see everything clearly'.

Some interpreters look for a medical explanation for the man's two-stage recovery of sight, but it helps if we remember that Mark uses healing stories as acted parables, signs of faith. Sight is a metaphor for faith (as it is in the later story of the healing of Bartimaeus in 10:46–52). Between the stories in 7:31—8:21 and here, the disciples have found it increasingly difficult to have faith in Jesus, despite all they have heard and seen. They need to have the ears and eyes of their hearts and minds opened, so that they can understand more fully about Jesus and his vision of God's kingdom.

Mark may intend this two-stage healing to be a sign of hope. If the disciples are currently 'deaf' and 'blind', the chances are that they will eventually come to 'hear' and 'see', though not instantaneously. Their faith will need time to develop, space in which to struggle with the uncertainties and contradictions that beset their attempts to follow Jesus. This message could hardly be more apposite. We are about to set out with the Twelve for Caesarea Philippi, where Peter will confess his faith in Jesus as God's Messiah, and Jesus will astound his disciples once more with his talk of the suffering of the Son of man.

Guidelines

In this week's reading, faith has been moving outwards, from the heart to parts of the world where some might not expect to find it. This movement of faith is only possible if faith is encouraged to grow, not least in quality and depth.

Recent research into faith shows that it changes and develops with us, as we move through life. A popular image is of the journey of faith, found in some modern baptismal liturgies. On this understanding, the development of faith is a natural process. Someone has said that faith is like a muscle: it grows strong by being stretched. This too is a natural process, but more stressful.

If the faith of the twelve disciples is to develop, it will need to be stretched like a muscle. Mark gives the impression of a constant stretching of their imagination, their beliefs about God and the salvation of Israel, their hopes for the future. Jesus is constantly surprising them, calling them to allow their faith to move and grow. Reading the Gospel can issue the same call to us. Where do we find growth difficult? What gets in the way?

Mark 8:27—9:50

I Faith and following

Mark 8:27–38

Alone now with the Twelve, Jesus has the chance to ask them the question that has long been swirling around in the story: 'What is this?' (1:27), 'Who can this be?' (4:41). Jesus moves gradually. How much popular opinion have they taken on board? However little they understand about Jesus, they do at least know what others are saying (v. 28). Then comes the direct question: 'and you, who do *you* say that I am?'

Peter speaks for the rest. His words echo the Gospel's opening line and the heavenly voice at Jesus' baptism. By now we know that messiahship can mislead. Hence Jesus' command to silence: he restricts all talk of 'the Christ' to the in-group. But there is a positive side to this: he wants to inform their (mis)understanding of his role and mission. 'Messiah' means different things to different people: leader of a revolution, restorer of the temple and its priesthood, heavenly judge who will make Jerusalem into the centre of a world empire. Jesus wants to lead the Twelve through their confusion to the true nature of *his* messianic vocation.

This is why he uses the surprising and shocking language of the 'son of man'. This messiah will fulfil his vocation as 'son of man'. A whole scholarly industry has grown up around the understanding of this term. Doubtless there are allusions to Daniel 7:13, and the vision of 'one like a human being' ('a son of man' in many translations) who is presented before the heavenly throne of God ('the Ancient of Years'). This 'son of man' represents 'the holy people of the Most High' (7:27), God's faithful ones who have been crushed by an oppressive and sacrilegious foreign ruler (thought to be the Syrian emperor Antiochus Epiphanes, who desecrated the temple in about 160BC). Daniel's vision is full of hope for God's faithful people. Despite their sufferings, God will vindicate their loyalty and reward them with his kingdom (7:27).

The prophet's vision is tailor-made as a vehicle for Jesus' faith and self-understanding. He will suffer, but not because this has any great virtue in the divine scheme. The enemies of God's kingdom—now seen as Israel's leaders, not foreign kings—will inflict their violence on him, but he will absorb it, and somehow use it to bring salvation to God's people. This is too much for Peter, who cannot imagine a messiah who allows his enemies to have such power over him. The Twelve will only understand Jesus' talk when they embrace his messianic way for themselves, as the sayings about discipleship show (vv. 34–37).

Jesus' words are unwelcome and uncomfortable. They reverse many conventional ideas—ancient as well as modern—about the way to overcome evil and build a better world. But as we shall see, they are crucial to what matters most: to be taken seriously, rather than regarded with shame.

2 Faith and listening

Mark 9:1–8

Jesus' faith in the power of God to vindicate his mission is so strong that he expects Daniel's vision to be fulfilled within a generation (v. 1). The saying has puzzled commentators, and perhaps even the evangelists. Matthew and Luke report it differently. Matthew 16:28 makes it refer to the coming of 'the Son of man in his kingdom', and Luke 9:27 leaves out the reference to the kingdom 'coming with power'.

Did Jesus expect a new world order to come soon? If so, he was wrong, and his followers would be disappointed. But for three of the Twelve, something does happen soon—within a week! The transfiguration is intended to convince these uncertain disciples that Jesus has the backing of the highest possible authority. Does this experience of heaven on earth anticipate what will come within a generation?

In Jewish tradition, the mountain is the locus of revelation, the place where heaven and earth meet. The brightness of Jesus' clothes—reminiscent of the Ancient of Years in Daniel 7:9—shows that heaven is open once more, as the glory of God floods Jesus with light. Like many Jews at the time, Peter and the others believed that Elijah and Moses were already in heaven. During their earthly lives, they were rejected by their people, but clearly not by God. The same will be true of Jesus: rejection by human authorities is no bar to recognition by God. The heavenly voice is a reminder of the words Jesus heard at his baptism. Now others are privy to divine speech, as God endorses all that Jesus has been saying about his messianic vocation. However difficult it is for these disciples to grasp Jesus' unexpected and disturbing way of being the Christ, they are to 'listen to him'.

It is understandable that the disciples should want a more permanent marker of their fleeting experience of heaven on earth. What they must grasp is that heaven and earth come together, not on a holy site, a preserve of pilgrims, a place to be disputed and even fought over, but in a way of living—the messianic way of redeeming the world revealed by this 'son of man' Christ.

3 Faith and resurrection

Mark 9:9–13

Once again Jesus forbids publicity. Impressionable people can easily be deceived by visions of heaven on earth. Notice that for the first time, Jesus puts a limit on silence: 'until the Son of man had risen from the dead'. Some scholars have wondered about the genuineness of Jesus' announcements of his resurrection. If he knew he would be raised from the dead 'three days afterwards' (8:31), would this not mitigate the horror of his suffering? If the disciples knew that his shame would soon be reversed, would they not be more easily able to cope with what was coming?

Sayings about resurrection might look like prophecy after the event, the fruit of reflection on what happened as a result of the death of Jesus rather than evidence of his foreknowledge. I have been suggesting that Jesus used the language of Daniel 7—'son of man', resurrection of the dead, the hope of a coming kingdom of God—to express his conviction that God would soon vindicate his cause: after three days, within a generation. Such was the strength of his faith that he could face whatever was coming, trusting that God would not abandon him in a shameful and violent death. Talk of an imminent resurrection is a natural expression of faith and trust, in the face of oppression and violence.

On their way down the mountain we find the disciples discussing what 'this "rising from the dead" could mean' (v. 10). Jesus is clearly investing familiar ideas and expectations with new meaning. What is he getting at? The question about Elijah is not a red herring. The scribes' teaching is based on Malachi 4.5. the prophet will come, presumably from heaven, to prepare Israel for the day of judgment. Early Christianity, prompted by Jesus, saw the fulfilment of Malachi's hopes in John the Baptist, whom Mark describes as an Elijah-like prophet (see the notes on 1:4–8). The link between Elijah old and new lies in what happened to them: 'they have done to him [the new] what they wanted, as the scriptures say of him [the old]'. Elijah suffered greatly at the hands of Israel, and Herodias succeeded where Jezebel failed (see 1 Kings 19:1–3). The lives of Elijah, John and Jesus are stamped by the same die.

This rising from the dead is more than a mere afterlife: it is the vindication of all that Jesus lived and died for. What might this mean for us today? Those whose lives are shaped by the faith of Jesus must always live with the disciples' question about resurrection.

4 Faith and prayer

Mark 9:14–29

When Moses came down from Mount Sinai after receiving the law, he was greeted by disarray among the people (Exodus 32). When he returned from the mountain a second time, his face shone and the people were afraid of him (Exodus 34:29–30). So Jesus, on his return from the mountain, encounters awe and disarray. Not this time idolatry among the people, but unbelief, particularly from his disciples, who struggle to heal the boy. We can share something of Jesus' amazement at their lack of faith, not least because on a previous occasion he has given them his authority to heal (see 6:6–13).

Matthew 17:15 describes the boy as 'an epileptic' (the Greek means 'moonstruck'). Western medicine would be horrified at any hint of demonic influence in epilepsy, but it is not hard to understand why the effects of an epileptic fit should be attributed to an invading evil power. Loss of speech, being thrown to the ground, convulsions, foaming at the mouth, grinding the teeth, rolling around on the floor before becoming rigid, loss of control such that water and fire were real risks to life—and all this since the boy was quite young. Demonic possession was a natural diagnosis for such life-threatening distress.

Can Jesus succeed where his disciples have failed? 'Everything is possible to one who believes' refers in the first instance to Jesus' faith. In his desperation the boy's father wants to share Jesus' confidence. His faith is tentative and uncertain (v. 24), but it is enough to leave him (and by extension his son) open to what Jesus can do for them. The healing is as traumatic as any fit: Jesus' word is met by 'repeated convulsions', and the boy is to all appearances dead. As with the daughter of Jairus, Jesus simply takes him by the hand. What follows is a kind of resurrection (v. 27; cf. 5:41–42).

Why had the disciples failed, when even the father's admittedly tentative faith had been enough to release Jesus' power to heal? Jesus' reply in verse 29 suggests that he is so open to God that his words to the unclean spirit are a kind of prayer. The incident reminds of the importance of faith and prayer in the way of this 'son of man' messiah. They—not swords and chariots—are the weapons with which the victory of God's kingdom is won.

5 Faith and children

Mark 9:30–41

Since 8:27, Jesus and the Twelve have been in the region north of Galilee. Now they are heading south, and Jesus wants to be undisturbed, so that he can devote himself to explaining to his disciples what it means for him to be a 'son of man' messiah. Doubtless they tell Jesus that they don't understand him. But they also display a silence that reminds us of the state of the boy in the previous story. Mentally and spiritually they are dumb, rigid, to all appearances dead.

Their sorry state is revealed in their topic of conversation on the journey. Jesus has been talking about the way that he is 'Christ', and the weapons he uses. But he has also been discussing the imminent coming of God's rule. The 'son of man' messiah will be vindicated within three days of his death. The kingdom will come with power within a generation.

So the Twelve can imagine themselves as a conquering army, on some kind of victory march to Jerusalem. Questions about rank and honour are uppermost in their minds. Jesus challenges them by reversing conventional wisdom and equating greatness with service. A child becomes an icon of true greatness. Children had low social status, and a high infant mortality rate and low life expectancy combined to consign them to the weakest and most vulnerable sections of society. For Jesus the little child stands for the power of God's kingdom to invert worldly estimates of honour, so much so that one who is weak and vulnerable can represent the Messiah, and even God (v. 37).

The Twelve also reveal their thoughts and attitudes in what they say about the follower of Jesus who does not belong to their group (v. 38). After their failure with the epileptic boy, there is a note of irony in their 'we tried to stop him'. An outsider is more successful than the insiders at healing in the name of Jesus. What Jesus asks of the Twelve is a measure of the conversion (or better, inversion) of heart and mind demanded by his messianic way. True greatness is measured not by a disciple's place in the 'in group', but by loyalty to one who can be represented by the lowliest and the least. What kind of faith does this demand of the followers of Jesus today?

6 Faith and single-mindedness

Mark 9:42–50

The sayings in this section are linked by catchwords. Those in verses 42–47 all contain the phrase 'cause the downfall'. Verses 48 and 49 are connected by 'fire', and the three sayings in verses 49 and 50 by 'salt'. It may be that Mark was responsible for joining the sayings; it is more likely that they had already been brought together before the evangelist knew them.

Verse 42 is concerned with undermining the faith of other disciples (followers of the Messiah who can be represented by a child are rightly called 'little ones'), and Jesus' warning could not be more severe. The millstone was turned by a donkey, and so was quite large. The next three sayings are about the perils of undermining one's own faith. There is some (disputed) evidence that amputation was used by the Jews as an alternative to the death penalty; it was certainly common in the surrounding nations. Again Jesus uses vivid exaggeration to make his point: better to be maimed than to enter hell whole! His language could hardly be more arresting, though it makes an interesting contrast with the teaching of the Essenes, for whom the maimed had no place in the kingdom of God. 'Hell' here is *Gehenna*, the Greek word for the Valley of Hinnon, Jerusalem's rubbish tip and formerly a place of child sacrifice to the god Moloch. Fire burned continually in a place whose atmosphere of decay, death and destruction is only highlighted by the quotation from Isaiah 66:24 in verse 48.

'Everyone will be salted by fire' is a difficult saying. Salt is a purifying agent and a preservative; fire in the preceding sayings refers to destruction. Paul writes of being 'saved through fire' in 1 Corinthians 3:15, and this may be the meaning here. The fires of judgment may not be entirely destructive: loss can be a means of gain, death a way to life (cf. 8:34–38).

Salt cannot lose its flavour and remain as salt. Perhaps Jesus refers to the salty deposits by the Dead Sea. Once the actual salt had been washed out of them, their 'saltness' would be no more. Disciples should make sure that their 'saltness' remains, and this is only possible if their faith is single-minded.

The final saying is again enigmatic. Does the first part ('you must have salt within yourselves') refer to maintaining the essential character of discipleship, or the readiness to share salt among the group of disciples? In view of the second part ('be at peace with one another'), the latter is more likely. Either way, Jesus warns against the divisive attitudes that prompted the arguments about greatness on the road to Capernaum. In the end they jeopardize faith, both within and beyond the community of Jesus' followers.

Guidelines

The further we read into the Gospel, the more we realize the power of Jesus to challenge and disturb. His own faith, and the faith he calls his disciples to live by, goes against the grain of so much in his world.

Sometimes Christian faith finds no problems in 'going with the flow', accommodating to the spirit of the age. In societies with a high level of material satisfaction, people are increasingly realizing that a vision of life that leaves no room for a spiritual dimension is inadequate and impoverished. Some of today's social and political aspirations—the desire for a more inclusive society, campaigns against world debt, care for the environment—find echoes in the concerns and hopes of Christian faith. But sometimes faith has to ask awkward questions about the way the world is. And that means 'going against the grain'.

Try looking through a magazine or a newspaper, or watching an evening's television, to identify where Christian faith can 'go with the flow', and where it has to 'go against the grain'.

Mark 10:1–52

1 Unconventional faith: marriage

Mark 10:1–12

Jesus and the Twelve leave Galilee and head south. After his talk of rejection, suffering and death at the hands of the Jewish leaders, he is now clearly on the way to Jerusalem and the final conflict. In much of the teaching in this chapter Jesus continues to challenge conventional assumptions about attitudes, beliefs and behaviour.

The source of the question about divorce is not clear—not all translations give it, because it is missing from some Greek manuscripts—though the reason is clear: 'the question was put to test him'. Moses permitted divorce (Deuteronomy 24:1–4), though Jewish scribes disagreed over the grounds. Some took a strict line and allowed divorce only if the wife committed adultery against her husband. Others were more liberal: as long as a husband issued his wife with a certificate of divorce, he could dispose of her if her cooking was inadequate. Where then does Jesus stand on this spectrum of interpretation?

He insists that Moses' permission—designed to protect the woman—should not obscure God's original intention: 'God made them male and female' (Genesis 1:27). 'That is why a man leaves his father and mother and is united to his wife, and the two become one flesh' (Genesis 2:24). Jesus strikes a body blow to the patriarchal system within which the divorce law operated. If 'male and female' are made in God's image (some rabbis taught that only the man was made in God's image, and the woman was made in the image of the man), and if husband and wife become 'one flesh' in marriage, a woman ought not be regarded as a man's property. He should not be allowed to dispose of her as he would a field or cattle. And if he does, and remarries, he commits adultery 'against her' (v. 11)—a startling statement, because under Jewish law adultery was committed against the husband whose property the woman was.

Jesus' teaching here is of a piece with his attitudes towards other disadvantaged groups. His vision of the kingdom of God challenges the idolatry of wealth and power, and feeds God's people with the bread of justice. It is as if Jesus wants to restore the ideal order of creation within Israel, something hinted at in his victory over Satan in the wilderness (see 1:12–13). So he forbids divorce where it is used as a way of oppressing women. (Verse 12 is likely to be a later addition, because under Jewish law women were not allowed to divorce their husbands; under Roman law they were.) In the messianic people of God, women and men are of equal value, and must be treated as such.

2 Unconventional faith: children

Mark 10:13–16

The discussion about relations between men and women leads naturally to the place of children. In view of Jesus' willingness to heal children (5:23–24; 7:26–30; 9:17–29), it is not surprising that he should be asked to bless them simply by touching. Why are the disciples so ready to rebuke those who make such an innocuous request? Their earlier discussions about status provide the clue (9:34). Then, Jesus used the low estate of the child as an icon of greatness and the epitome of humility. Here he welcomes and receives little children in all their vulnerability and weakness.

Notice how Jesus is angered by the disciples' rebuke. Matthew 19:13–15 and Luke 18:15–17 make no mention of Jesus' indignation —perhaps they are reluctant to criticize the Twelve. But for Mark, this is clearly an issue worthy of arousing strong feelings. 'The kingdom of God belongs to such as these' echoes Jesus' teaching in the first Beatitude (Matthew 5:3), and informs our understanding of what it might mean to receive the kingdom 'like a child'. Children are examples of those who are 'poor in spirit'. Such people have no hope other than God, and so they are able to receive his blessing as a gift. This cuts through human preoccupations with honour or status. The kingdom of God is freely available to all, irrespective of human estimates of worth. On this understanding Jesus issues yet another sharp challenge to those who divide and rule the world according to conventional values.

Alternatively we might interpret 'as a child' as 'receiving God's kingdom as one might receive a child'. In other words, disciples must allow the Messiah's inversion of worldly values to give a new shape to basic social relations and the attitudes that undergird them. The messianic way goes against the grain of conventional estimates of honour and status, inclusion and exclusion. If women and men belong equally to the restored people of God, then so do children and adults.

There is little to choose between these alternatives and their practical consequences. Once again Jesus comes across as a man of unconventional faith, and his messianic way as challenging, disturbing, even subversive.

3 Unconventional faith: wealth

Here is a man who treats Jesus with the utmost respect, kneeling before him in recognition of the honour due to a 'good teacher'. It is easy to misunderstand the substance of his question. REB translates it as 'what must I do to *win* eternal life?', which suggests something to be earned rather than received. RSV follows the Greek more closely: 'what must I do to *inherit* eternal life?', that is, to enter into what God has promised to his people. 'Eternal life' literally means 'life of the age', life in the coming new world (notice how the verses that follow equate 'eternal life' with 'entering the kingdom' and 'being saved'— vv. 23, 26, 30). So the man is asking about how he can share in the blessings of the time of salvation, the kingdom of God that is drawing near in the ministry of Jesus.

Jesus is uneasy about being called 'good', and points to God as the source of his authority as a teacher. (Notice how Matthew 19:16–17 alters this: Jesus is simply 'teacher', and replies to the man with 'why do you ask me about what is good?' Is this a sign of Matthew's embarrassment at Jesus' apparent self-deprecation?) As one whose actions and teachings always express the will of God, Jesus naturally refers the man to the law of Moses. Notice that he avoids those parts of the law that deal with issues of purity (food, sabbath, and the rest), in favour of the commandments—though not all of them. He leaves out the first four, which deal with the worship of God, and replaces the last—'you shall not covet'—with 'do not defraud' (this is only found in Mark's version of the story).

Jesus probes below the surface of the man's claim to an upright life. No one should underestimate what he asks him to do. To sell his family home and land, to break his kinship ties, to abandon all earthly security and join Jesus' band of disciples is a tall order. Jesus demands nothing of him that he has not already asked of the Twelve—to take his place with the least rather than the greatest, the servants rather than the served. His sorrowful departure shows that he is one in whom 'the false glamour of wealth... chokes the word' (4:19). And if covetousness is a form of idolatry (Colossians 3:5), he is a man who has made an idol of his wealth and power.

4 Unconventional faith: persecutions

Mark 10:23–31

Jesus' reflections on his encounter with the rich man are reserved for the disciples. They are understandably alarmed by his statement about wealth as a hindrance to receiving the blessings of God's coming kingdom. Conventional wisdom saw wealth as a sign of God's favour. These words from Proverbs 3:1–2 are typical of this outlook:

> My son, do not forget my teaching,
> but treasure my commandments in your heart;
> for long life and years in plenty
> and abundant prosperity will they bring you.

If the wealthy enjoy God's blessings now, surely they will do so all the more in the age to come.

Jesus' repeated 'how hard' is driven home by his saying about the camel passing through the eye of a needle. Some commentators completely miss the point by trying to minimize the absurdity of the image—replacing 'camel' (Greek *kamelos*) by 'rope' (Greek *kamilos*), or suggesting that 'the eye of a needle' is a (completely unknown) gate in the walls of Jerusalem. Jesus uses exaggeration and humour to make the point that the kingdom of God subverts divisive estimates of human worth, even when these are based on the scriptures! He sees beyond the trappings of wealth to its dangers. Wealth and power seduce people into worshipping their place in the world, rather than God. And those who idolize wealth and power will do all they can to preserve their privileged status—which means keeping the poor, the weak and the vulnerable at arm's length.

What about the disciples, then, who have done what the rich man was not prepared to do? Jesus reminds them of the blessings that are already theirs. Like him, they may have abandoned family and traditional ways of earning a living, but they have gained a wider family in the community of faith, and are not deprived of the means of life. The reference to persecutions—which are diametrically opposed to prosperity, and so run counter to ideas about divine blessing—may have been inserted by Mark to reflect the experience of his audience (it is not found in Matthew or Luke). Even persecutions cannot detract from the blessings of salvation, as Jesus' own experience will demonstrate. If the first (the conventionally privileged) are to be last when God's kingdom arrives, the last really are the first to enjoy a world that is at last starting to reflect its creator's intention.

5 Unconventional faith: power

Mark 10:32–45

This is now the third time Jesus speaks of what lies ahead in Jerusalem, and the details are more precise. He will not merely be rejected by the Jewish leaders, but 'handed over' to them (a hint at his betrayal by Judas), and condemned to death. The Gentiles (the Roman occupying forces) now have a part to play, in inflicting on Jesus the insults and torture reserved for the enemies of Rome. Doubtless the wording is influenced by the actual course of events. But Jesus does not need supernatural insight to gauge the likely outcome of taking his vision of God's reign to the symbolic centre of Israel's life and identity. He needs only to remember the fate of the prophets who came before him.

The request of James and John for positions of power and influence shows that Jesus' words about status and honour continue to be lost, even on his leading disciples. They are clearly rejecting the advice of the heavenly voice at the transfiguration (9:7). There is heavy irony in their demands following so closely on the heels of Jesus' most explicit statement about his passion. They still cannot see that his is not the traditional messianic role of the warrior king.

Even Jesus' recourse to the imagery of 'cup' and 'baptism' makes little impression. The cup is a picture of suffering (see Psalm 78:5), and baptism suggests the power of water to drown and destroy, as in the story of Noah. Jesus expects to meet his end in a calamitous flood of violence that will engulf Israel should his messianic way be rejected. And if there are overtones of divine judgment in these images, then Jesus may see his own death, rather than the destruction of Israel's enemies, as somehow cleansing the world in preparation for the coming age of salvation. How can James and John tell Jesus that they have it within them to embrace what is coming to him? Their bravado will soon be exposed as a reckless overestimate of the capabilities of the whole group.

Jesus goes on to remind the Twelve of his earlier words about the inversion of status, honour and power in God's kingdom. As Son of man, he is the complete antithesis of those Gentile rulers who idolize their power by using it against their subjects. Those who walk the messianic way with him must be willing to use what power they have for the benefit of others, not at their expense. Who better to exemplify this way of liberation from the destructive cycles of violence than 'the Son of man who did not come to be served but to serve, and to give his life as a ransom for many' (v. 45)?

Jesus' final response to the issues raised by James and John underlines the cost of walking the messianic way. His unconventional faith will enable him to go on giving his life to set others free from oppressive forms of power, until he has no more to give. And as Son of man, he does not expect to walk alone (cf. 8:34–38).

6 Unconventional faith: vision

Mark 10:46–52

In Jericho now, Jesus and his band draw nearer to Jerusalem. As if to demonstrate his redeeming power, he heals the blind beggar Bartimaeus. The last time Jesus opened the eyes of a blind man was in 8:22–26, just before his first passion prediction. Once again Mark uses sight as a metaphor for faith. By placing this story here, at the end of a long sequence of teaching about Jesus' surprising and unconventional way of being the messiah, Mark shows how it is that the eyes of faith are opened.

Bartimaeus is reduced to begging by his blindness—he is therefore poor. He uses a conventional messianic title ('Son of David') to attract Jesus' attention, though he has to struggle for a hearing. We can picture him by the roadside, all but overwhelmed by the noisy crowd. By now we are not surprised that Jesus notices him. Bartimaeus is like the children and women we met earlier—weak and vulnerable in a world that wants to use its power against them, but in the eyes of Jesus they have as much right as anyone else to the blessings of God's kingdom.

'What do you want me to do for you?' might seem an unnecessary question, but it shows Jesus' willingness to serve the man (cf. 10:45). 'Rabbi' here is *rabbouni*, a more reverential form of address than Peter uses in 9:5 and 11:21, and an expression of faith—faith that allows Bartimaeus to receive the blessings of salvation ('healed' in v. 52 translates the Greek word for 'saved').

Then comes the most significant part of the story. Bartimaeus, who now sees, becomes a disciple. Notice the small but significant touches with which Mark colours the story. In verse 49, Jesus tells the crowd to '*call* him', and for their part they tell Bartimaeus, 'take heart, get up, he is *calling* you'. Then in verse 52, with his faith affirmed and his sight restored, he '*followed* Jesus on the road'. A poor man does what a rich man could not do (10:17–22). And he answers Peter's earlier question about who can be saved (10:26). Coming so soon after the persistent spiritual blindness of the Twelve, Bartimaeus is a sign of hope that those who have followed Jesus all the way from Galilee might come to 'see' the messianic significance of Jesus' self-giving. But only as they follow him still further to Jerusalem are the eyes of their faith eventually opened.

Guidelines

Last week's Guideline invited you to think about 'going with the flow' and 'going against the grain'. The titles of this week's readings have drawn attention to the non-conformist element in much of Jesus' faith.

Mark is keen to impress on his readers that Christian faith is more than mere belief. It is not simply a matter of using the right words about Jesus ('You are the Christ'), or even just following him around. Christian faith is certainly inspired by the faith of Jesus, but even this is not enough. The faith Jesus looks for is nothing less than the willingness to identify with him, however unconventional his visions and values may be.

We reach the end of these readings in Mark as Advent starts. You might like to begin your spiritual preparation for Christmas by asking yourself about the element of *identification* in your faith. In what ways do you identify with the God who comes to the world in the birth, teachings, actions, passion and vindication of Jesus?

WOMEN IN THE BIBLE

In Advent we wait to be surprised again by God. It might seem strange for us to be reading about some of the women in the Bible as part of our preparation for Christmas. But, of course, when that great festival comes, our thoughts will be centred on a woman, as well as on a child, a Jewish woman from a nowhere of a place in first-century Galilee called Nazareth. It will be good to put her in the company of other women from the Bible, from both Testaments. She has been buried beneath layers of piety and devotion. We will try to unearth her and rediscover some of her features. It will help us to do that if we have already brought to life some of her biblical sisters.

We will be speaking of some women whose stories have been thoroughly distorted in the church. We will discover others whose stories have been almost entirely neglected. We will come across poetry of stunning quality, which is only beginning to be recognized as the work of women. We will find pathos and humour, pain and defiance, stories to encourage us, stories to provide us with some holy disturbance.

We will devote the first week of readings to women in the Old Testament, the second to women from the New. We will end, appropriately, with Mary of Nazareth.

The Bible version we have used is the NRSV, but any reputable translation will do for your own study.

3–9 DECEMBER

From the Garden of Eden to the Song of Songs

1 The woman in the garden: an innocent abroad

Genesis 3:1–12

Women in the history of the church have suffered more from this passage than any other in the Bible. The woman in the garden of Eden is a temptress, so we are told, who leads her man astray into challenging God and trying to gain his power. After she gives him the fruit of the forbidden tree, everything falls apart. The harmony of the garden is destroyed, its easy pickings replaced by thorns and thistles. It is all her fault. The man says so, at 3:12.

But let us make a few things clear. The language of temptation is missing. 'She gave some to her husband, who was with her, and he ate.' That is all. No fluttering of eyelashes on her part, and no reluctance on his.

Second, at this point in the story the 'woman' and 'man' are emotionally little more than children, and small children at that. Through eating the fruit they come to recognize they are different from one another, and looking at one another, they are suddenly overtaken with teenage embarrassment (the story has them growing up rather fast!). By the time the story ends they will know all too well what adult life involves.

Third, the woman, or the little girl, is not trying to storm God's kingdom when she takes the fruit of the forbidden tree. Verse 6 explains her motives. Encouraged by the snake, she looks at the tree and sees nothing special about it. Like the other trees in the garden (see 2:9), it is 'good for food', 'an attraction to the eyes', and 'a delight to consider' (my translation). So, of course, she and the boy can take its fruit.

The snake has effectively cancelled out God's command. So they eat. And what is the result? Not all the world's ills. They simply grow up too fast, and God cannot keep them safe in his garden any more, nor secure in the innocence of childhood. They must leave the garden and move on to the uncertainties and the trials of the adult world.

The woman in the garden is not a temptress—more an innocent abroad.

2 Hagar: the one who gives God a name

Genesis 16

Some of the women in the Bible are rich and hold positions of power. Sarah is one of them. Others live on the edge of their societies, and seem to have no power or wealth at all. Hagar is among those. In Sarah's and Abraham's household she is a foreigner, an Egyptian. And she is a slave. According to Genesis 12:16 Abraham had acquired many male and female slaves in Egypt, but we hear nothing of the others here, nor in Hagar's other story in Genesis 21. It is as if she is quite alone, with no one to turn to. Abraham shows her a measure of concern in chapter 21. He shows her none at all here, but treats her purely as his sexual property, and hands her back to Sarah's bitter tyranny without hesitating. Because she is a slave, the child she is carrying will not count as hers, but will belong to her mistress.

And so, abused, fearing perhaps for her life and the life of her unborn child, she runs away, and makes for Egypt. Like other runaways, she is caught and returned to her mistress. To our alarm, the one who stops her and brings her bid for freedom to an end is God himself.

And yet this same God tells her that freedom will in due time be hers, and her child's also. And this God (or the storyteller, if you prefer) allows her an annunciation scene, the first of a handful of such scenes in the Bible. Sarah, her mistress, will not have one for Isaac. And she, Hagar, *sees* God. Only a very few people in the Bible do that in so many words. Jacob does, and Moses, and Isaiah. Not Sarah, not even Abraham. *And* she gives God a name. No one else in all scripture does that!

So this runaway foreign slave, this abused woman, bearing a child of a man who does not love her, and which she will not be allowed to keep, this desperate woman, alone in the harshness of the desert, finds herself crossing the threshold of heaven, and leaves God with a love-token of a name to hang round his neck and remind him of her!

What remarkable hope this story contains!

3 Shiphrah and Puah: making a fool out of a god-king
Exodus 1:8–22

Now the boot is on the other foot. Now Israelite is at the mercy of Egyptian. And that Egyptian shows no mercy at all. In its place there is racial hatred and violence, fuelled by the usual paranoia and whipped up by a vicious tyrant. It is a sadly familiar picture. These ancestors of the Jews are not quite in Auschwitz, but they are in the gulag all right.

When the two heroines of this story, Shiphrah and Puah, come on the scene, things get even worse. Pharaoh has decided upon a policy of genocide, and Shiprah and Puah are to implement it. In the original Hebrew it is not clear whether the women are Israelites or Egyptians. But they are definitely midwives. Their work is delivering women, bringing babies into the light of the world, helping them take their first breaths of air and cry their first cries. Now they are ordered to become agents of death, stopping the breath in babies' throats, smothering them to a fearful stillness.

They do not argue with Pharaoh. How could they? They simply ignore his orders. Yet he has his informants, and summons the two women once more to his throne room. In Egypt a pharaoh was worshipped as a god. How can these women stand up to him? They are guilty as charged. How can they possibly survive?

By telling a joke! They tell Pharaoh the Hebrew women are 'vigorous' and give birth before they can get to them. In the original Hebrew the word for 'vigorous' sounds like the word for animals. 'These Hebrew women,' they say in effect, 'are like animals, your majesty! They just drop their babies and go on their way! We can never get there quickly enough!'

Pharaoh believes them! They come away from the palace unscathed, and Pharaoh gives up on midwives and gets the general populace to do his dirty work for him instead.

Shiphrah and Puah's story is one of inspiring courage, cleverness (see how their joke appeals to Pharaoh's racism and sexism) and quick thinking. It is also a story of inspiring faith. For these two women are able to stand up to Pharaoh and his terror because of their overriding loyalty towards God.

4 Rahab: living on the edge

Joshua 2:1–16

Another woman on the edge of her society, literally this time, as well as metaphorically. Not only is she a prostitute, but her house is set within the walls round Jericho. As a prostitute she is a used and abused woman, and again like Hagar, she is in great danger. A people is on the move and Rahab's ancient city lies within their promised land. By the terms of Deuteronomy (see 20:16–18), they are commanded by God to annihilate the towns of the land, letting nothing that breathes in them remain alive. And Rahab knows nothing can stand in the way of this God.

Then she has a stroke of luck. Two spies from the Israelite camp knock on her door. Gary Cooper, John Wayne, Clint Eastwood and James Bond have all used brothels as safe houses at one time or another. These two Israelites do the same. But they have been spotted! Another knock on the door. The king's men. The spies are hidden beneath piles of flax on the roof. Rahab fobs off the men at her door with an outright lie. Instead of searching the house, they rush off through the town gates. Now she seizes her chance. She does a deal with the spies, to save her own skin when the time comes, and the lives of the members of her family.

With Shiphrah and Puah, she belongs to the company of female tricksters in the Bible, clever women who make fools out of men, in her case the men sent by her king. She is also among the faithful outsiders, the remarkable band of Gentiles who possess a clear understanding of the ways of the God of Israel, people such as Uriah in 2 Samuel 11, or the Syrophoenician woman in Mark 7. It is possible that behind Rahab's tale lies a fragment of a different account of the destruction of Jericho, one that spoke of her enabling a stealthy entry and the town's capture from the inside. Certainly her survival in Joshua 6 makes little sense in that story of the walls falling down flat, since her house is set within them. Whatever the case, for her own people in Jericho she is a traitor, who plays a significant part in their ruin.

Her story has elements of the plot of a classic spy thriller, and is not without its humour. But it also contains the disturbing presentation of a God who engages in what we would describe today as ethnic cleansing.

5 Job's wife: a pain unheeded

Job 2:1–10

Women are more conspicuous in the Bible as a whole by their absence. Where, for example, is Sarah in the famous story of the binding of Isaac in Genesis 22? And where is Job's wife in the long tale of his misery, his protests, his vision of God and his restoration? Only here, in this one passage. And she only has, in the Hebrew, six words to say!

She has lost almost everything. Her wealth has gone, her means of support, her position as one of the leading women in the village, her *children*, *all* of them. Only her husband is left to her, but he is sitting on the village rubbish dump, apparently dying from a vicious skin disease. What of *her* grief, *her* anguish, *her* loneliness? Job the character, and Job the book, seem to pay them no heed whatsoever. She is dismissed by Job as a silly woman, and given a pious answer that makes a mockery of that true religious faith which looks reality in the face (compare Job's reply with Jesus' agonized pleading in Gethsemane—Mark 14: 35–36).

And yet, when she opens her mouth, we hear an authentic, human voice. Her six words are charged with an agony we can recognize at once. By contrast, the Job of these opening two chapters seems unreal, impossibly good. It is not until we enter the poetry of the third chapter that we hear Job releasing his emotions—angry, bewildered, crying out his soul to a God he feels has treated him most cruelly. His wife with her six words brings us back to earth, and despite his initial response, they bring her husband back to reality also. She succeeds in opening the floodgates of his anguish. She plays a much larger role in the book than first meets the eye.

6 The poetry of love, the poetry of women

Song of Songs 8:6–7

There is some material in the Bible openly attributed to women, such as the Song of Deborah in Judges 5, or the words that king Lemuel was taught by his mother in Proverbs 31 (see verse 1). But there is other material, such as Proverbs 1–9, or the book of Lamentations, which may also come from female sources, and that is so with the Song of Songs.

This wonderful collection of secular love songs, celebrating the delights of sexual love, is believed by many scholars to have come from women. The poems reflect women's experiences; they assert the equality of the sexes and the dignity of women; they protest against cramping, loveless conventions, designed by men to protect their own interests; and while they are split between a woman's voice and a man's, it is the woman's which predominates. The poets who first sang these songs, and the laments of Lamentations also, and who lie behind the early chapters of Proverbs, are, we suggest, the hidden women of the Bible.

The famous little poem in 8:6–7, spoken by the woman, celebrates the power of love to defeat death itself, or even the waters of Chaos that threaten to engulf God's creation. It contains a veiled protest against the custom of arranged marriages, whereby the men of the family decided whom their daughters or their sisters should marry, and decided upon the bride price. Yet the poem begins with something very small and intimate, a person's seal, worn round the neck and against the heart, or else on the wrist or the arm. A seal was often made of precious stones and metals, and it spoke of the person who owned it, and carried their identity. 'Set me as a seal upon your heart.'

In just four words in the Hebrew the poet captures the preciousness of lovers to each other, their intimacy, their making their mark upon one another, their finding in their love for one another and their union a new identity. In just four words she has captured the mystery of romantic love! Pure genius!

Guidelines

The trouble with women in the Bible is that there are not enough of them (even if we allow for hidden women authors in places), and those who are there tend to play bit-parts. The Bible is largely made up of material composed by men, reflecting men's values and their concerns, as well as their assumptions about their innate superiority.

Admittedly, in the long narrative that stretches from the beginning of Genesis to the end of Kings, women have a habit of turning up at key moments—the woman in the garden of Eden, Sarah, Rebekah, Rachel and Leah, Shiphrah and Puah, Rahab in Jericho, Hannah at the start of 1 Samuel, Bathsheba at the turning point of the long story of David. And yet both Testaments, coming as they do from patriarchal societies, neglect almost entirely the spiritual life of women. No woman in the Old Testament receives a commission to do some great work for God. No woman in the Gospels is bidden by Jesus to follow him. The stories we have about women in the Bible may often be compelling, but they only serve to remind us of how much is not told.

From one Mary to another

1 Mary of Magdala: Jesus' most devoted follower?

John 20:1–18

What do we know about this Mary? She came from a prosperous fishing town on the western side of the Sea of Galilee, called Magdala. She first met Jesus when she was ill. Luke tells us she had been possessed by seven demons (8:2). That suggests the illness had completely taken her over. Jesus cured her, and she became one of his inner circle, leaving everything behind to follow him (Luke 8:3). We suspect it was highly unusual, if not scandalous, for a woman to accompany an itinerant preacher in such a way.

More important still, she saw Jesus crucified. Mark, Matthew and Luke all speak of three of his women followers standing at a distance. Their names for these women vary, but each of them includes Mary of Magdala. John alone describes one of the male followers and Jesus' mother being there. But he also tells of three other women, among them Mary of Magdala. So all four Gospels agree: Mary of Magdala did not run away; she heard the nails; she saw Jesus die. If people ask who first told the story of the cross, we have to answer, 'Well, Mary of Magdala, for starters.'

All the Gospels are agreed on another thing: Mary of Magdala was among the first witnesses of the resurrection. Their lists of those who went to the tomb that first Easter morning do not agree, but Mary's name occurs in all of them. In John's famous story she alone goes to the tomb without prompting, and she is the one who cannot tear herself away from it. As a result, she is the first to meet the risen Jesus.

Like Hagar, Moses or Paul, she encounters the divine in all its mystery. Alone of all the women in scripture, she is then given a divine commission—to tell the good news of the resurrection. In John, she is the first preacher of the gospel.

Why then do the letters of Paul and the book of Acts say nothing about her? Her devotion to Jesus had been second to none. What part must she must have played in the early church?

2 An unnamed woman with a haemorrhage

Mark 5:21–34

We do not know this woman's name. Yet we know enough about her to realize something of her calamity. For twelve years she had suffered from uterine bleeding. As a Jew she had been ritually unclean all that time. During that time she would have been unable to have children, too. Jewish custom and religious law would have meant her husband would have had to divorce her. She was allowed out of the house, of course, but she was supposed to avoid crowds, for fear of touching someone by mistake. Religious law claimed that she could make someone ritually unclean just by brushing against their clothes. She would have been terribly anaemic—also, as weak as a kitten. She was destitute, ostracized, on her own, tired out and in pain.

Understandably, she has no self-confidence. She dare not approach Jesus directly. She comes up behind him in the crowd and reaches out for his clothes. A girl is dying, and Jesus is on his way to her. But, no doubt, she thinks Jesus will not notice anything. She is not going to stop him and ask him to heal her. She is only going to touch his clothes. He is a holy man, a prophet, a man of God. Just a touch will be enough. But immediately Jesus turns. For a moment her weakness has become his, and his strength has disappeared into her.

Why does Jesus stop and speak to her? Because he wishes to reassure her that she has not made him unclean. And he wishes to reassure her in public, so that the crowd knows she has done nothing wrong. His words are meant for those around this woman, as well as for her. 'This poor woman's desperate need is more important than your religious scruples,' he is saying to them.

116

But he is telling them more than that. The woman knows she is well. But the people of the town need to know that, too, and they need to know that from his lips. Her condition has isolated her from them for twelve years. Now she can rejoin the community, and it is their task to welcome her back, to remove her fear (and her poverty). Jesus tells her 'to go in peace'. It will be the task of her community to make sure that peace comes to reality. Jesus' work is done. He must go on to other things and to other people, to a house full of grief and a dead girl. The work of the woman's community has only just begun.

3 This time a foreigner

Mark 7:24–30

Another desperate woman, only this time it is her daughter she is concerned about. We do not know what is wrong with the girl. The woman says she has a demon. That does not mean she is what we would call mentally ill, only that the illness did not have any obvious, outward cause. The only clue is given right at the end of the story, where the healed girl is described lying quietly on her bed. Was she too distraught with pain before? Was she uncontrollable? We shall never know.

But we do know the woman was not a Jew. We know also that she breaks all the rules by entering the house where Jesus is lodging in the way she does. By the customs of her day she insults the family to which the house belongs. She insults Jesus' own people, the Jews, by assuming she can share their privileges and have her daughter healed. She insults Jesus' male honour by entering his presence without any invitation. She ignores all the strict rules of hospitality and how women should behave before men. In the eyes of those who first heard Mark's story Jesus' rebuke would not only have been understandable, it would have been expected. 'Shameless hussy!' they would have said. 'Who does she think she is? Quite right, Jesus!'

Yet his rebuff is not the end of the story. The woman persists. For Mark's hearers that would have made her more shameless still. But she is driven, of course, by her desperate need and the needs of her child, by her love for her daughter. Nothing else matters. She will not take 'no' for an answer. So she argues—and Jesus accepts her argument and heals her child. She is the only person in the Gospels to get the better of Jesus in an argument.

But winning arguments is not what this story, nor this woman, is about. Her persistence opens Jesus' eyes. No longer is he shocked by her shamelessness. Instead he sees before him a woman who loves her child, who is desperate for help, and who believes he can provide it. She is not a Jew, but that has suddenly become irrelevant. He had thought his task was primarily to save his own people, make them once more truly God's people (though see Isaiah 49:6). This woman, who, if she was a contemporary of ours, we would call a Lebanese Muslim, is conscious that human need knows no boundaries. Everyone belongs to God and needs God's life and wholeness. She is one of the great heroines of the Bible.

4 On the edge of destitution: a widow in the temple
Mark 12:41–44

A poor widow who gives the rich scribes a lesson in generosity, and a Jesus who points her out admiringly to his friends. That is the way this story has usually been heard. However, there is another way of looking at it, for that interpretation does not take into account the context in which Mark places the story. It comes immediately after harsh words from Jesus about the scribes, members of the religious establishment, 'devouring widows' houses', and not long after his condemnation of the temple as 'a den of robbers'.

This Jesus has come on pilgrimage to Jerusalem after spending much of his time among the poor of Galilee. He has told stories about the men who have to stand around the market place every day, hoping they will have something to take home to their wives and children at the end of it. He has been confronted by people like that woman with her haemorrhage, ostracized and completely destitute.

He himself came from a small peasant village, and from a family where Joseph could not earn enough from the land to keep them all, but had to do odd jobs as a carpenter to survive. The poor were among his most devoted followers.

Now they have come with him to the Jerusalem temple, the dwelling place of God, the heart of divine generosity, the place above all places where justice should be found, where dreams of 'life as a watered garden' (as Jeremiah described it) should be turned into reality.

And what does he find? A temple which drains the poor dry, where men count more than women, people from Jerusalem more than peasants from the north. He watches as the women put their offerings into the trumpet-shaped chests placed round the walls of the Court of the Women.

He sees the widow, sees her very clearly, sees she now has nothing left, sees how she will have to beg on the streets or else starve to death. She should have gone away from the house of her God with her pockets bulging, pushing a wheelbarrow full of goodies. Instead, she who arrived on the edge of destitution leaves completely destitute. And far from lost in admiration, Jesus is full of indignation, angry with a place and its authorities who could do such a thing to her.

5 Another widow, another persistent woman

Luke 18:1–8

We turn now to another needy woman, the persistent widow in Jesus' parable of the unjust judge. The focus of the parable is chiefly on the judge, but we can still work out enough about this woman. Her husband has died, and she has no sons to look after her, otherwise they would certainly have approached the judge on her behalf. So she is extremely vulnerable and quite possibly among the very poor.

The Bible in both Testaments bears eloquent witness to how hard lives could be for such women. Yesterday we saw an example from Mark. To make matters worse, this particular widow has been done some wrong. Jesus does not tell us what it is, but it is serious enough for her to make repeated attempts to gain justice, and to keep bashing her head against what must seem a brick wall. Someone is obviously making life very difficult for her. Is her opponent making a false claim on her property? Has he trumped up some false charge against her, so that she has been ostracized by her community? We cannot tell. We are left to imagine.

The trouble is the judge she appeals to has no justice in him. He has no time for *God*, so it is hardly likely he will have any for a widow who is on her own with no one to support her. But, like so many of Jesus' parables, the story has a twist. In the end the judge is afraid for his honour. He lives in a society where male honour is almost more precious than life. He cannot let this woman destroy his good name. 'I will grant her justice,' he says, 'so that her coming does not end up putting me to shame.' (That is probably what the end of verse 5 means.) So he settles her case. He has not changed his spots, only reviewed what is in his own interests.

'Compare that judge with God!' says Jesus. 'God has such a passion for justice, and such a keen eye for oppression! We do not even have to knock on his door! Take a good look at it! It has no lock, no catch, even. Its hinges are well-oiled. A touch and it swings open. So do not lose heart!'

6 Mary of Nazareth—not as subservient as she seems
Luke 1:26–38

Pictures can speak louder than words. This meeting between Mary and the angel has been painted over and over again. Some of the most exquisite paintings in the great galleries of the world are of this scene. Yet they tend to pay little heed to the terms of the story, and to reflect much more clearly what the church came to make of Mary in the centuries after the Bible was written.

Rarely, if ever, do they show Mary's origins. In Matthew's Gospel, her home town was Bethlehem. Here in Luke's it is Nazareth, a very small, obscure peasant village in the Galilee hills. Mary came from a peasant family in an occupied country.

Very rarely if ever do the paintings of Mary, or Miriam, to give her Hebrew name, reveal she was a Jew. Later she would have taught her son the stories of Hagar, of Rahab, of Abraham and Sarah and Moses. She would have taught him not the teachings of the Sermon on the Mount, but those of that more ancient mountain, called Sinai.

Rarely do they reveal her age. She would have been betrothed to Joseph when she was about twelve.

Often they interpret the angel's words about the Holy Spirit 'coming upon her' and 'overshadowing her' as referring to the moment of conception. But those phrases are familiar to us from the Old Testament. They do not indicate conception, but empowerment and protection.

And they do not capture her spirit, as we find it in Luke's account. The song she sings soon after this passage, the song we call 'the Magnificat', is a defiant, subversive song of triumph, full of energy and hope, crying aloud a faith in a God who is on the side of the nobodies in the world, and who topples oppressors from their places of high power.

Above all, perhaps, they have not caught the pride in those words of hers in our passage, 'Here am I, the servant of the Lord; let it be with me according to your word.' They have portrayed her as meek, submissive and subservient.

At first blush that is what Luke's words seem to make her. Indeed, the Greek is stronger than our English versions. It speaks of her as God's *slave*. And yet, if we again refer back to the Old Testament, we find Abraham being described as God's slave, and Moses and David, and Hannah, too, Samuel's mother, and the prophets.

And the Roman empire of Miriam's own day was administered by slaves of the emperor, some of the most powerful men around. In calling herself God's slave this peasant women puts herself in very exalted company, and declares herself a member of God's household, no less, part of God's entourage! This young Jewish girl tosses her head with a pride she had never dreamed of!

Guidelines

There is much good news for us in the stories we have discussed these past two weeks, much to inspire and encourage us, whether we are women or men. But we are discomfited, also. If we are men, we will find some of these stories challenging our assumptions, our stereotypes, the values of our still male-dominated society. If we are women, then the stories may challenge us not to play men's games, but to claim our rightful, God-given place and dignity.

All of us need to remember the astonishing claim of the Old

Testament that all human beings, women as well as men, are made in God's image and likeness (see Genesis 1:26–27). That was royal language, language that kings in the ancient near east reserved for themselves. The poet of Genesis 1 declares we *all* have royal status, given to us by God at our creation! And we need to remember also those fine words we find in Paul's letter to the Galatians: 'There is no longer Jew or Greek, there is no longer slave or free, *there is no longer male and female*; for all of you are one in Christ Jesus.'

O Servant God,
come with a broom in your hands
and sweep our minds and our hearts clean
of the dirt of prejudice,
of cramping assumptions and narrow stereotypes,
of unnecessary guilt, and low estimations of our worth.
Make us spick and span,
ready to receive you this Christmastide.
And receiving you,
may we share the vision of Hagar,
the courage and loyalty of Shiphrah and Puah,
the love and devotion of Mary of Magdala,
the proper pride of Mary of Nazareth,
to your great glory,
O Servant God. Amen.

FURTHER READING

Trevor Dennis, *Sarah Laughed: Women's Voices in the Old Testament*, SPCK, 1994

Margaret Hebblethwaite, *Six New Gospels: New Testament Women Tell their Stories*, Geoffrey Chapman, 1994

Carol A. Newsom and Sharon H. Ringe, eds, *The Women's Bible Commentary*, SPCK, 1992

SONGS OF GLORY

Praise the Lord! How good it is to sing praises to our God. (Psalm 147:1)

At this time of year, thousands of people will discover this for themselves in churches all round the world. The familiar songs of Christmas can seem trite and meaningless when we hear them in a supermarket or on a TV advert. But when we sing them in a carol service or a packed midnight mass, they take on another quality altogether. In a communal act of worship they draw out what is personal to us—our memories, our joys, our sorrows—and make it part of something far larger and greater. Our stories become interwoven with those of our neighbours, and with the central story of the Son of God born in our midst. And as we sing those stories together it becomes both an offering to God, and a discovery of God. As the shepherds learned long ago, the glory of God can touch our lives at such moments.

Over the next two weeks we will be exploring the glory of Christmas by looking at the four songs which Luke includes in his story of Jesus' birth: Mary's Magnificat, Zechariah's Benedictus, the Gloria of the angelic host, and Simeon's Nunc Dimittis. (The traditional titles come from the opening words of the songs in Latin.) Although Luke describes them as being spoken rather than sung, they strongly resemble the hymns and sacred songs of the Jewish scriptures. It seems that Luke consciously used this style as a way of bringing the past, present and future together. The songs remember Israel's longing for salvation, and their dreams of a better world. They celebrate the way this is coming to fruition in the birth of the long-awaited Messiah. And they look forward to a world transformed by the knowledge of God's saving love for all people.

These are songs of praise. But they are also songs of prophecy, which challenge us to work for the transformation of our own world until the justice and peace of God become a reality for everyone.

These notes are based on the New Revised Standard Version (NRSV), but they may be used with any version of the Bible.

The Magnificat and the Benedictus

I The Magnificat: setting the scene

Luke 1:26–38

Reading the annunciation scene as a prelude to the Magnificat can shed new light on a familiar story. Several key themes are established early on. First, the 'favour' of God is declared to Mary (vv. 28, 30). As we shall see, this idea dominates all four songs, and the circle of favour is enlarged at every stage until it includes everyone, Jew and Gentile alike. The arrival of the Messiah is not a judgment on humanity, but rather an expression of God's continuing delight with us. The creator continues to look on all that is made, and finds it good. No wonder Mary rejoices.

Second, the promises of God are being fulfilled in a surprising way. The Saviour of the world will grow secretly in Mary's womb, his greatness framed and shaped by her humility (vv. 31–33). The Magnificat—and indeed the rest of the Gospel—will celebrate this irony again and again, as conventional notions of power and greatness are completely overturned in Jesus' life and teaching. The Messiah from the house of David was expected to repeat David's successes, winning great military victories which would re-establish Israel as the powerful and prosperous nation they had once been. Yet this son of David would usher in a very different kind of kingdom, the kingdom of peace prophesied in Isaiah 9:7, rooted in the justice and righteousness of God.

The other central theme is the greatness of God. Here God is named as the Most High, the Lord (vv. 32, 35)—again, terms that contrast sharply with the lowly circumstances of the child's birth. This is the God that Mary will celebrate in song. Our word for worship is derived from the Old English *weorthscipe*, reflecting the 'worth' of the one who is worshipped. As Mary shows, true worship involves obedience as well as praise, for only then do we allow God to be God. Her voluntary surrender to the will of God will be mirrored later in the Gospel as her son wrestles with his fears in Gethsemane (22:42).

2 The Magnificat: celebrating the greatness of God

Luke 1:46–50

'My soul magnifies the Lord!' As we saw yesterday, worship defines our relationship with God. God is great, and is 'made great' (the literal meaning of the Greek word) by our praise. But where does that leave us? It is important not to let our own sense of unworthiness prevent us enjoying God's gifts.

Mary finds the right balance. Although she acknowledges her lowly state, she recognizes and fully accepts the grace of God for what it is. God has looked on her with favour (v. 48) and done great things for her (v. 50). And if all generations should call her blessed as a result, so be it. How do we feel about the blessings we enjoy? And how is that reflected, both in our prayers and in our lives?

In hymns of this style, the opening declaration of praise is swiftly followed by a statement setting out the reasons for it (vv. 49–50). Two particular qualities of God are identified here—holiness and mercy— and they form another theme which Luke develops carefully in his Gospel. He is particularly fond of stories which seem to contrast the two virtues: Simon the Pharisee and the woman who anoints Jesus' feet (7:36–50); the two brothers in the story of the Prodigal Son (15:11–32); the Pharisee and the tax collector (18:9–14). In each case, the presence of mercy exposes the 'holiness' as a false and narrow self-righteousness. In reality, the holiness of God is merciful, and the mercy of God is holy.

These are not only moral attributes. As Psalm 111 shows, Jewish thought often linked both qualities with concrete acts of liberation:

The Lord is gracious and merciful:
he provides food for those who fear him. (Psalm 111:4–5)

He sent redemption to his people;
he has commanded his covenant forever:
holy and awesome is his name. (Psalm 111:9)

We shall see tomorrow how Mary continues to explore this theme.

3 The Magnificat: celebrating the new world order

Luke 1:51–55

As the song moves outwards in scope, Mary's own experience becomes a key to exploring the wider activity of God. God has always intervened to help the lowly (vv. 51–52). The Greek verbs speak of decisive action in the past. Although no specific examples are given, the song echoes those psalms which celebrate Israel's exodus from Egypt and other occasions of deliverance (e.g. Psalms 114, 118, 137). There are also clear parallels with Hannah's song in 1 Samuel 2:1–10.

This is where the prophetic tone of the Magnificat comes to the fore. Like Hannah, Mary sets up a series of comparisons which celebrate the radical displacement of the proud, powerful and wealthy in favour of the poor and powerless (vv. 52–53). Again, this is seen in very concrete terms: 'God has lifted up the lowly; he has filled the hungry with good things, and sent the rich away empty.' Despite Luke's use of the past tense, this will also be a hallmark of Jesus' ministry (see 9:12–17, 18:18–25) and of the continuing ministry of his followers (see 14:7–14).

As Mary says, the promises of God are there for every generation (vv. 54–55). So how can we implement that radical vision in our own age? At a time of year when the gulf between rich and poor can be all too apparent, how will we respond to the real needs around us?

These can be uncomfortable questions in a relatively wealthy society. But Mary's song reminds us that our individual experience of God cannot be separated from the overall vision of justice, health and peace that is promised in the kingdom of God.

4 The Benedictus: setting the scene

Luke 1:5–25, 39–45, 57–66

As the length of today's reading illustrates, Luke attaches great importance to the story of John's birth. But it is clear at every stage that John is the forerunner, not the main act. Even though he will be 'great in the sight of the Lord' and 'filled with the Holy Spirit' (v. 15), his main task will be to 'make ready a people prepared for the Lord' (v. 17—the prophecy of Isaiah 40:3).

This is a prophetic role. In this respect, John is likened both to Samuel, who prepared the way for David, and to Elijah, who was expected to return before the Messiah came. Like Samuel, John will be born to a barren woman, and abstain from strong drink (see 1 Samuel 1:1–11); like Elijah, he will preach the way of righteousness, and 'turn the hearts of parents to their children'. According to Malachi 4:5–6 this would herald the 'great and terrible day of the Lord'. Although John's preaching will reflect this note of judgment, it will do so in order to prompt repentance (see 3:7–9). Gabriel's message is 'good news' (v. 19).

The similarities between the two stories—the appearance of Gabriel, the miraculous conceptions, the giving of names—allow us to contrast the reactions of Zechariah, Elizabeth and Mary, and learn from their experience. Zechariah's doubts are understandable; like Abraham and Sarah (Genesis 17:16–17) he finds it difficult to believe that a son can be born to such elderly parents. Yet to their great joy it is true. Elizabeth rejoices immediately (vv. 25, 41–45), and her joy and her grasp of the situation clearly help both Mary (vv. 36–38) and Zechariah (vv. 60–63). Experiences of God are given to be shared.

Zechariah regains his speech only when he insists that the child is named John, in fulfilment of the angel's command (vv. 13, 63). It is his act of obedience which sets him free to glorify God (v. 64).

5 The Benedictus: celebrating the faithfulness of God

Luke 1:67–75

Zechariah's song begins where Mary's ends, celebrating the fulfilment of God's promises to Israel. In a sense, the song is about the future. As he promised, God has now raised up a Saviour from the house of David (vv. 69–70). Yet this is interpreted according to the great acts of salvation that Israel has known in the past.

Again, the exodus is seen as the central event. This is where the people were most dramatically redeemed (v. 68) and saved from their enemies (v. 71). As we can see from Psalm 106, the ancient songs of Israel looked back to this moment in times of trouble, and found in it a reminder of God's constant love and loyalty:

He rebuked the Red Sea, and delivered them
from the hand of the enemy. (Psalm 106:9–10)

Many times he delivered them, and showed compassion
according to the abundance of his steadfast love. (Psalm 106:43–45)

Zechariah traces the roots of this steadfast love back to God's covenant with Abraham (vv. 72–73). As Genesis 17:1–10 makes clear, a covenant involves a pledge by both parties. Here, the response to God's saving initiative is that we should 'serve him without fear, in holiness and righteousness before him all our days' (vv. 74–75). For Zechariah, a temple priest, this would naturally involve formal worship (the Greek verb carries the sense of priestly service).

This is an important theme for Luke, who begins and ends his story in the temple. But there are also implications for our life in the world. This time holiness is linked with righteousness, or justice (the same Greek word may mean both)—and it is this aspect of God's promise that will be addressed in tomorrow's reading.

6 The Benedictus: celebrating the dawn

Luke 1:76–79

For two verses Zechariah focuses on the role his son will play in the unfolding drama. He will be the prophet of the Most High (v. 76), the one preparing the way for the Lord. As we saw earlier, this refers back to the prophecy of Isaiah 40:3, but the same idea also appears in Malachi 3:1 concerning the anticipated return of Elijah.

All the Gospels go out of their way to stress that John is not the Messiah, which suggests that there may have been confusion or conflict at some point. Luke makes the point very simply: John is the prophet of the Most High, whereas Jesus is the Son of the Most High (v. 32).

John's role will be an important one, however, for he will 'give knowledge of salvation to his people by the forgiveness of their sins' (v. 77). Luke is very different from Matthew in this respect. In

Matthew, John calls people to repentance, and baptizes them as they make their confession (3:1–6). The implication is that Jesus alone can forgive sins. Yet Luke follows Mark in making John an agent of forgiveness as well (see Mark 1:4). As the Jewish scriptures remind us, it is God who forgives sins, as he has always done: 'To the Lord our God belong mercy and forgiveness' (Daniel 9:9).

The Messiah's role and purpose is broader than that. As Zechariah outlines it in verses 78–79, it is a blaze of light into a world darkened by suffering and death. The image comes from Isaiah 9:2, where the prophet looks forward to an endless kingdom of peace, freedom and justice. We will hear more about peace next week, when we look at the angels' song. In the meantime, it is important that those who dwell in darkness and the shadow of death should not be forgotten at Christmas. In our prayers and in our actions, how can we help bring the light of Christ to them?

Guidelines

As we have seen this week, both the Magnificat and the Benedictus celebrate the divine plan of salvation that is coming to fruition in Christ. In the midst of their celebration, however, they examine closely what that salvation really means. This is why the harsh realities of life are never far from the surface. Poverty and hunger, suffering and death —this is where people need salvation, in the real issues which confront them in their day-to-day lives.

Later in the Gospel, Jesus will make the same point about himself by reading out Isaiah 61:1–2 and declaring, 'Today this scripture has been fulfilled in your hearing' (4:16–21). The poor will hear good news; the captive will be released; the blind will see, and the oppressed will go free. The child in these songs and the firebrand in the synagogue at Nazareth are one and the same person.

Sadly, some of our Christmas songs can be cloyingly sentimental, and lead us away from that kind of vision of reality. But the best songs bring together the deepest needs of the world and the highest hopes of heaven, and as they do so, they encourage us to look for the glory of God in both places:

Yet with the woes of sin and strife
The world has suffered long;
Beneath the angel-strain have rolled
Two thousand years of wrong;
And man at war with man, hears not
The love-song which they bring:
O hush the noise, ye men of strife,
And hear the angels sing.
EDMUND SEARS (1810–76)

(Next week's Guideline suggests listening to some of the ways in which these four songs have been set to music. No particular composers are recommended, as musical tastes vary so widely. The idea is that you should find something which inspires you. You may already have your own favourites, but if not, you may like to spend some time in a library or record shop this week, sampling some of the options.)

24–30 DECEMBER

The Gloria and the Nunc Dimittis

1 The Gloria: setting the scene

Luke 2:1–7

Such are the purposes of God that even the emperor of Rome unknowingly plays his part in the drama of salvation. According to Luke, Augustus' census ensures that Jesus is born in Bethlehem, the ancient home of the house of David (see Micah 5:2).

'He will be great, and will be called the Son of the Most High, and the Lord God will give to him the throne of his ancestor David' (1:32). Gabriel's words have prepared us for a royal birth, surrounded with awe and wonder and majesty. Yet the reality could not be more prosaic. Mary's labour comes quickly; the town is full; and the incarnate Son of God must spend his first night in an animals' feeding trough.

'Foxes have holes, and birds have nests; but the Son of Man has nowhere to lie down and rest' (9:58). Luke makes much of Jesus' homelessness. Even in death, he will be laid in a stranger's tomb (23:50–53). And yet he is not without comfort. Then, as now, he will be wrapped in cloth by those who love him. That simple act speaks volumes about the mystery of the incarnation. First, the Son of God experienced human need. As the figure of Solomon comments in the apocryphal book of Wisdom: 'I was nursed with care in swaddling cloths. For no king ever had a different beginning of existence. There is for all one entrance into life and one way out' (Wisdom 7:4–6). Second, and more significant, he also experienced those needs being met. The source of all love knew what it was to be loved, not only by God, but by the people who filled his life.

The needs of that new and highly vulnerable baby remind us of those in our own world who are in need of shelter, warmth and comfort. In a sense, providing financial or prayerful support is the easy option. It is much harder to provide practical, tangible help; and yet that is what this story challenges us to do.

2 The Gloria: celebrating the glory and peace of God

Luke 2:8–14

The true splendour and majesty of Jesus' birth, hidden in yesterday's reading, now bursts out as the angel appears to the startled shepherds. As glory of the Lord shone around them (v. 9), the message of salvation is announced. The universal 'good news of great joy for all the people' (v. 10) is also directed personally to the shepherds: 'to you is born this day' (v. 11). The child is not just a Saviour; he is their Saviour—and ours, too.

Jesus is also described as the Messiah, and the Lord. Luke may simply be stringing the different titles together, just as he did in 1:32–33, to denote Jesus' overwhelming greatness. But it is possible that the titles follow a deliberate sequence: Jesus is hailed as the Saviour of particular individuals or groups, like the shepherds; he is hailed as the Messiah of Israel, the Chosen One for the chosen people of God; and he is hailed in universal terms as the Lord of all.

This sense of an ever-widening picture continues as the angelic host lift their voices in praise: 'Glory to God in the highest heaven, and on earth peace among those whom he favours!' While the earlier songs had spoken of God's favour resting on Mary (1:48), and on Israel (1:68), this time there are no limits. The God of highest heaven is the God of the whole earth; and the peace of God is offered to everyone through the gift of this child.

As we saw last week, this peace (in Hebrew, *shalom*) includes justice and righteousness (Isaiah 9:1–7), but that is only part of the vision sketched out in the early chapters of Isaiah. True shalom also embraces political harmony (Isaiah 2:4), economic harmony (3:13–23), and social and ecological harmony (11:1–9). Here again, the song of praise is a song of prophecy, setting out the transformative quality of the kingdom which is dawning in Christ.

3 Reactions to the Gloria

Luke 2:15–20

The shorter songs this week allow us to see how the leading characters in the story respond to all they have seen and heard.

Recognizing that 'the Lord' has spoken to them through the angels' words, the shepherds set off for Bethlehem immediately (v. 15). Unlike the disciples who witness Jesus' transfiguration (9:28–36), they have no desire to hold on to the glimpse of glory they have experienced. It has been enough. In all that glory, they have recognized that the focal point is something far more mundane—a child wrapped in cloth, lying in a manger (v. 12)—and that is what they hasten to find (v. 16).

As the shepherds repeat the angel's message to Mary and Joseph (v. 17), they offer a classic model of evangelism. Quite literally, they are handing on the 'good news' they have received (v. 10), news which amazes everyone who hears it (v. 18). Luke will record a similar sense of amazement many times as Jesus' ministry gets under way (see, for example, 4:22, 32, 36).

Mary seems less amazed (v. 19)—presumably because she has already heard the good news from both Gabriel and Elizabeth. None the less, she treasures the shepherds' words, and ponders them in her heart. Luke's portrait of Mary is very reflective at this point. It is an invitation to the reader to meditate on the angels' message, to think about the meaning of Christ's birth, to explore its implications in our own day and age. Mary has already proved herself to be an outstandingly receptive and faithful disciple, and yet even she has more to learn. As we read again the familiar words of the Christmas story, may we too find fresh meaning in it.

4 The Nunc Dimittis: setting the scene

Luke 2:21–28

Luke is keen to show how Jesus' parents comply with the requirements of Jewish law, so Jesus is circumcised and named (after eight days, as in Leviticus 12:3), and Mary is purified (presumably after 40 days, as in Leviticus 12:1–8). However, the purification seems to be conflated with another ritual, where Jesus is presented to the Lord. This may be modelled on the consecration of the first-born required by Exodus 13:2. But it is interesting that Luke does not mention the ritual 'buying back' of the first-born which is stipulated later in that chapter.

Again, there are echoes of the story of Hannah and Samuel (1 Samuel 1:11, 24–38)—Mary and Joseph do not buy back their son, because they are handing him over to God. When Jesus later speaks of his 'father's house' on another visit to the temple (v. 49), it will be transparently clear whose child he is.

It is a huge sacrifice on Mary and Joseph's part, and its full significance will only begin to emerge as Simeon speaks of the child's future (vv. 34–35). We will look more closely at that in two days' time, but it is important to note here that the faithful obedience shown by Mary and Joseph applies equally to the law of Moses (v. 22), and to the word of God which Gabriel has spoken (1:31, 35).

From verse 25, the focus switches to Simeon. Among the many qualities Luke mentions, it is his openness to the Holy Spirit— mentioned three times—which stands out. In traditional Jewish thought, this marked him out as a prophet (see, for example, 1 Samuel

10:10–12), and his specific prophetic role was to recognize the Messiah (v. 26). As this suggests, speech is only one aspect of prophecy. The gift of discernment is equally important—the ability to be in the right place at the right time; the ability to see things for what they are; the ability to recognize in them the hand and voice of God. How can we be more open to the Spirit in all these things?

5 The Nunc Dimittis: celebrating the revelation of God
Luke 2:28–32

As Simeon takes the Christ-child in his arms, there is a profound moment of recognition. The Spirit's promise—that Simeon would not see death until he had seen the Lord's Messiah—is now fulfilled (v. 26).

The granting of that promise means Simeon's song begins on a slightly strange note. It is a song of praise, as Luke points out (v. 28), and yet the first thing Simeon praises God for is the fact that he can now die. We do not know how old he was, or how long he had waited, but what is clear from verse 29 is the deep sense of peace that he feels at the prospect. This, too, is part of the shalom of God.

In the same verse, Simeon uses the traditional Greek words for master and slave to describe his relationship with God. It is a mark of the devotion which Luke has already mentioned (v. 25), but it also illustrates why he has such peace. Like Mary and Zechariah before him, he is content to allow God to be God, in death as well as life.

The song moves on to explore the hope of salvation encapsulated in this tiny child. Based on an earlier prophecy of Isaiah, that hope is explicitly universal: 'The Lord has bared his holy arm before the eyes of all the nations; and all the ends of the earth shall see the salvation of our God' (Isaiah 52:10).

It is this child who will be the light (v. 32), bringing revelation to the Gentiles, and glory to Israel. In this context, revelation and glory appear to have the same meaning—Jews and Gentiles alike will see in Christ the presence of God, and be saved by it.

The breadth of Simeon's vision is thought-provoking. Is everyone saved, simply because this child has been born? Or is there more to it than that? However we answer these questions, it is important to hear the hope and confidence of Simeon's song.

6 Reactions to the Nunc Dimittis

Luke 2:33–35

It is difficult to know why Mary and Joseph are 'amazed' at Simeon's words (v. 33), given all they have seen and heard before. Perhaps it is the universalism of his vision; perhaps it is just the coincidence of yet another stranger recognizing who their son is. In fact, what follows seems more remarkable, because it is here we get our first glimpse of the future that lies in store for this child.

Simeon offers a mixed blessing, to say the least (vv. 34–35). When he speaks of Jesus being 'destined for the falling and rising of many in Israel', it is clear that his ministry will have a disturbing and unsettling effect. The image may stem from Isaiah 8:14–15, where the prophet speaks of Israel falling down after knocking against the stumbling-block of God. Later, Luke connects this idea with Psalm 118:22: 'What then does this text mean, "The stone that the builders rejected has become the chief cornerstone."? Everyone who falls on that stone will be broken to pieces' (Luke 20:17–18).

The sheer fact of Jesus forces people to choose. Is he the Messiah, or is he not? Many will oppose him, and all will find their thoughts revealed as the 'light'—Simeon's term for Christ (v. 32)—shines into their hearts. Yet according to his prophecy they will also rise. Ultimately, it seems to be a hopeful message for the people of Israel.

For Mary, however, it is a dark and difficult message: 'A sword will pierce your own soul too'. Her son will also have his falling before he discovers what it is to rise. This could refer to the rejection which Simeon has just mentioned; it could also refer to his ultimate fate. Even at this early stage, the shadow of the cross is glimpsed in the narrative.

Guidelines

After so many words, it is time we allowed the music of these songs to speak to us. Whatever song(s) you have chosen, in whatever setting, play them several times, and allow yourself to hear in the music some of the hopes, the dreams and the glory we have thought about for the last two weeks. If you find your thoughts wandering into other areas of life, stay with those thoughts, for there too the glory of God can break through in our midst.

Music can be a discovery of God. It can also be our offering to God. Above all, let the music help you rejoice in the story of the Saviour's birth. And as we stand on the threshold of a new year, let it help you celebrate the dawning of God's reign of peace throughout our world.

For lo! the days are hastening on,
By prophet bards foretold,
When with the ever-circling years,
Comes round the age of gold;
When peace shall over all the earth
Its ancient splendours fling,
And the whole world give back the song
Which now the angels sing.

EDMUND SEARS (1810–76)

FURTHER READING

Richard Burridge, *Four Gospels—One Jesus?*, SPCK, 1994

Robert C. Tannehill, *The Narrative Unity of Luke–Acts*, Fortress, 1986

Guidelines

Magazine

Preachers—born or made?

Stephen Wright

Is it really possible to teach people how to preach, or how to preach better? Isn't it a gift that you either have or you haven't? When people ask me this, it comes quite close to the bone! My main business is trying to help people, directly or indirectly, to learn to preach, or to preach better. And I do it because I passionately believe it is possible.

Let me get the qualifications out of the way first. Yes, of course some have a particular gift in preaching. Yes, there is something deeply personal about preaching. Yes, prayer is a vital component. Yes, we have no wish to squeeze preachers into a particular mould. And yes, there are a few preachers who, for whatever reason, would struggle to benefit from any attempt to help them do it better.

Nevertheless, would-be preachers *can* be trained and existing ones helped. How? And how might the College of Preachers be able to contribute?

Friendship and feedback

It seems obvious to say that to receive friendly support, encouragement and comment is one of the main ways in which we can grow as preachers. Yet this is one of the main things that is often lacking! Both in initial preaching training, and in our continuing preaching ministry, preachers can be caught in a culture of isolated individualism. This can feed pride, fear of criticism, and loneliness.

There is a growing recognition that if preachers are to develop to their full potential, preaching needs to be seen as far more of a corporate enterprise than it has been. As bonds of trust are built among preachers and between preachers and listeners, the individual's particular gift of preaching can be nurtured, problems larger or smaller surmounted, and all that is good affirmed.

The ways in which these bonds can grow are many. The key is that all who preach should be involved in some continuing, honest dialogue about how they are being heard and how they can use their gift to the full. It seems ludicrous that we should go on from month to month, year to year, in some cases perhaps even decade to decade, without this kind of serious engagement. Which one of us really wants to cut ourselves off from Christian fellowship and openness when it comes to an activity that demands such energy and vulnerability?

Ideally, all who preach regularly would be in a group of local preachers and listeners that met regularly for the specific purpose of reflecting on the ongoing preaching ministry in that place. Looking back, looking ahead; talking over ways of handling lectionary texts or church festivals; offering constructive critique and support. Clearly, the degree of usefulness of such gatherings would be in direct relation to the degree of trust among their members.

Some might think that this diminishes the sacredness of preaching. Isn't God's working through preaching a mystery, which can't be discussed and dissected? However, the fact that it is a mystery shouldn't stop us helping each other in our human task, but should make us sensitive to its awesome dimensions. In his book *Surviving the Sermon*, David Schlafer has some very helpful guidelines for groups that meet to reflect on preaching, which enable us to move beyond the level of crude judgment ('What did you think of X's sermon on Sunday?') to discerning the way in which Spirit, speaker and hearers are playing their part, and how the speaker might play his or her part in future.

The College's courses and conferences, local, regional and national, offer an opportunity for fellowship in preaching ministry. We are able to respond to requests for training tailored to a particular group—or, indeed, for personal advice. At some events there is the opportunity for participants to preach short sermons and receive feedback in the kind of supportive group just mentioned.

And we can do more! Members of the College at the moment receive a twice-yearly Journal, a valued resource for forty years, which will continue its important role. But we work now in an informal environment. Keeping in touch with others is much easier than it was. We want to develop links between members for mutual encouragement and practical ideas concerning preaching, through e-mail and small gatherings. This is the kind of vibrant, informal College that we want to become, and which readers of these notes—whether preachers or keen listeners!—can help bring to birth.

Feeding the minds

Perhaps one reason why we have found it hard to give and receive serious feedback on sermons is that we haven't had the opportunity to think through what it is that makes for effective preaching. So, when all the vicar can think of to say to the curate about his or her sermon was, 'That was good' or, 'Something seemed to be missing there', it may not be for lack of desire to help, but lack of the right tools for thinking about preaching.

The fact is that much theological training in the UK has neglected the study of preaching. It is sometimes assumed that knowledge of scripture and Christian doctrine will ensure good preaching. It does not.

Preaching is a proper object of study in itself. This does not mean that learning to preach is a matter of simply learning some rhetorical techniques. It means grappling with the need to *connect* God's calling to us to preach the gospel, teach the faith and interpret the scriptures with all the practical things about communication that we can learn from writers, artists, dramatists, journalists and so on. It means seeking out wisdom from God's word *and* God's world, and finding the relationship between the two which will enable us to pass on his message in authentic fashion.

There has been a wealth of creative thinking about preaching recently, especially in America. This is far from being uniform or monochrome, and there is lively debate. The College seeks to further this debate and 'feed the minds' of preachers, through the Journal and through its events. It is a mark of a living church and preacher to be continually reflecting on our calling.

The College is also now able to offer accredited courses in preaching via open learning. The Certificate in Theology (Preaching) is a foundation course with the needs of beginners, or would-be beginners, in mind. Most of the nine modules (on subjects such as 'Basic Preaching Skills' or 'The Mission Context of Preaching') will be available by autumn 2001. The Masters in Theology (Preaching) is for those who have done initial theological study, and preached for some years. It opens up significant current trends—in contemporary culture and in the interpretation of scripture—to keep preachers equipped.

> *Preaching that makes its mark involves creativity*

Nurturing the creative spirit

Preaching that makes its mark involves creativity. Every preacher knows what it is to 'run dry'. This comes not only from tiredness and pressure, but also from not being in touch with the sources of renewal within and around us.

I acknowledged earlier that preaching is a very personal business. Unfortunately, some draw the conclusion from this that when we're not inspired, there's nothing we can do about it. Actually, we can do something. Precisely because it's a personal business, we should be nurturing those aspects of ourselves that help to make us, as unique individuals, most alive.

It's a strange thing that the person from whom some of the most regular, fresh, inspiring input is demanded—the preacher—is often the one so overburdened with duties that there seems little opportunity to 'come up for air'. Whatever activities make us feel most ourselves—sport or music-making or swimming or stitching —we should count among our most important commitments.

More specifically, we can nourish our preaching by both looking in and looking around. Looking into our own experiences, drawing from the wells of our memories, we can discover a sense of God's meaning in the world that will make the earthing of our preaching genuine rather than secondhand. Being in touch with ourselves, we will be at ease in preaching, not trying to emulate a style that is alien to us. Looking around, we find an endless store of created things that can ignite the spark afresh inside.

Another function of the College's Journal is to point to and awaken these sources of life. The sermons that we print are not intended as substitutes for the preacher's own creativity, but catalysts for it—as, we hope, are the articles and reviews too. Our gatherings also can richly fulfil this purpose.

If you are a preacher, can I invite you to join us by becoming a member of the College? Or if you are a regular listener to sermons, who is concerned to have the very best, what about giving membership to your minister or someone else who preaches in your church? Through friendly feedback, mental stimulation and nurturing of creativity, the gift of preaching can be fanned into flame, and preachers can go on learning and growing. Through membership of the College, you will be doing more than supporting what may seem a worthy but rather distant cause, and receiving some resources for yourself. You will become a part of an ecumenical fellowship which together can foster encouraged preachers and dynamic preaching in our churches.

The gift of preaching can be fanned into flame

For details about membership and all activities, please contact The Administrator, Mrs Karen Atkin, 10a North Street, Bourne, Lincolnshire PE10 9AB. Tel/Fax: 01778 422929. E-mail: collpreach@mistral.co.uk You can also visit us at www3.mistral.co.uk/collpreach

Stephen Wright comes from Northumberland and worked as an Anglican priest in Cumbria and County Durham for eleven years before becoming Director of the College of Preachers in 1998. He is the author of The Voice of Jesus: Studies in the Interpretation of Six Gospel Parables, *published by Paternoster in 2000.*

An extract from
Living the Gospel

So much of the teaching of St Francis challenges the values of today's consumer-driven culture. Yet while he remains an enduringly popular figure, St Clare, an early follower and teacher of his values, is far less well known. *Living the Gospel* looks at St Francis and St Clare together, showing how they shared responsibility for the growth and influence of the Franciscan order, and how deeply rooted their teaching was in scripture. Author Helen Julian CSF has been a member of the Community of St Francis for 16 years and is Guardian of St Francis Convent in Somerset.

The relationship of equality implied in being brother and sister informed the model of community life which Francis and Clare both lived and commended to their followers. Clare was particularly radical for her time. In most religious communities of the day the Abbot or Abbess was a powerful figure, rather remote, often living apart from the other members of the community, in considerably better conditions. But, as we have seen, at San Damiano it was only with great difficulty that Clare was persuaded to become Abbess at all, and she remained entirely part of the community. Visitors to San Damiano today are shown the corner of the communal dormitory where she

> *Clare was particularly radical for her time*

slept, and the record of the canonization process is full of stories of how she humbly served her sisters. Her Rule provided that new members could only be admitted, or debts incurred, with the agreement of all the sisters. Each week a meeting was to be held to discuss the life of the house, and all the sisters from the oldest to the youngest could have their say. The Abbess and the other office holders could be removed from their office at any time by the sisters of the house, acting together. All authority came from the group, and the Abbess was the servant of the sisters. In fact she was to be so accessible to them that they could speak to her as 'ladies do with their servant'.

Francis also provided that those in charge (the guardians and ministers) should be servants of all the brothers. He too cared for the brothers he lived with, and did not expect to be treated differently because he was the founder of the community. But a firm structure was needed to hold together the brothers in their itinerant way of life, and so Francis legislated for a rather more hierarchical, less democratic system of authority than that which Clare set up at San Damiano, where the sisters were together constantly, and could therefore consult regularly as an entire group. The brothers came together only a few times a year, and as the order grew these meetings were huge, with several thousand brothers gathering from all over Italy and further afield.

But always Jesus was the model. 'I did not come to be served but to serve' (cf Matt. 20:28) introduces a brief admonition by Francis which should give all those in positions of authority pause for thought. Francis instructs them that they should only be as glad about such a position as they would be if given the job of washing their brothers' feet. And if they are more upset about losing such an office than they would be about losing the job of foot washing, then their souls are in peril. It seems that for Francis, the key to the right use of authority is not to seek it out or cling to it; for Clare, the key is to share it.

But for both, authority is best exercised as service. The words which Francis uses tell their own story. Nowhere does he speak or write of superiors; instead those in positions of responsibility are ministers, custodians or guardians. In the Early Rule we read: 'And no one should be called Prior, but all generally should be called Friars Minor [that is lesser brothers]. And the one should wash the feet of the others.' That this made great demands on those given responsibilities can be seen in Francis' *Letter to a Minister*. We don't know who the recipient was, but from the letter know that he was in charge of a province of brothers, was having a lot of trouble from them, and wanted to retire to a hermitage, abandoning such a difficult job. Francis wrote to encourage him to continue, to love those who were making his life difficult, and not to wish for them to be better Christians.

> *For Francis, the key to the right use of authority is not to seek it out or cling to it; for Clare, the key is to share it*

What applied inside the community also applied outside. The brothers who worked (which in the early days was probably most of them) were not to be in powerful positions. They were to be labourers or servants, not treasurers, overseers, administrators, managers or supervisors. From equality he would have them move to 'minority'—to be the lesser ones (cf. Luke 22:26), following Christ who was 'as one who serves' (Luke 22:27). Far from being in control of others, they were to be dependent on others.

Within the community too relationship was central. The sisters at San Damiano, and the brothers in their scattered communities, were not just separate individuals, each pursuing their life of prayer, or of preaching and service. They were to treat each other as family. 'And wherever the brothers may be together or meet [other] brothers, let them give witness that they are members of one family.

Using very feminine language, Francis uses the picture of a mother caring for her son to describe the kind of care which the brothers are to have for each other. He spells out what this means in terms of behaviour; primarily, they are to love not only in word but in deed (1 John 3:18). So they are not to quarrel or become angry with each other. Neither are they to speak about another brother behind his back, or to spread gossip. They should not become obsessed by the small faults of each other (easier said than done when living with people one has not chosen), but stay aware of their own faults and weaknesses. Thus they will not judge each other.

Clare too, in her Rule, warns the sisters to guard against 'pride, vainglory, envy, greed, worldly care and anxiety, detraction and murmuring, dissension and division'. Both Francis and Clare were very realistic about the difficulties of living together, and the daily struggle necessary to preserve 'the unity of mutual love, which is the bond of perfection'. Thomas of Celano witnesses that such unity did exist at San Damiano. Writing four years after the death of Francis, he says that although there are forty or fifty sisters living together (and San Damiano is not a large place), their mutual love binds their wills together and makes them of one mind and spirit.

To order a copy of this book, please turn to the order form on page 159.

An extract from
What's Wrong

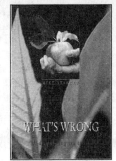

In this stimulating new study, Mike Starkey revisits the whole idea of sin. He tackles head-on the objections to believing in sin, but also challenges the way believers have sometimes presented it to others. The result is a fresh and powerful restatement of the historic Christian understanding of what's wrong with the world. Mike is vicar of Holy Trinity, Twickenham in west London. His most recent books include *God, Sex & Generation X* (1997) and *Restoring the Wonder* (1999).

What we are, objectively, is people 'in Christ', adopted, justified, liberated—the whole package. That is how Paul can claim that believers have 'died to sin' (Romans 6:2), and been set free from sin (Romans 6:18). This is quite true, in the sense that sin no longer causes the road-block between us and God. On the cross on Good Friday, sin was put to death. In the empty tomb on Easter Monday, humanity was raised to new life. And we can participate in that new life simply by saying 'Yes' to it.

Equally anybody committed to living the Christian life knows for themselves how hard it can be. Sin may have been conquered, but we still live in a fallen world. We still struggle with doubt, alienation, bad habits, distorted relationships. The tempter is still at large. We participate in structures of injustice and oppression. The challenge for me,

as a believer, is to become in daily reality what I already am in the eyes of God. Some days I make good progress, victory seems close, and the Christian life has its moments of pure ecstasy. Other days I slip backwards, and feel an utter failure.

One thing is for sure: this struggle to uproot sin is a lifetime's job. Sometimes the struggle will seem so hard that I might feel like giving up altogether. But I am not in this alone. I have all the resources of God himself at my disposal, and there are fellow pilgrims along the way to share my burdens.

Feeding snakes

Let's be honest. To some people, all our talk of mutual support, imitating Christ, the power of the Spirit, self-discipline and so on will sound fine in theory. Many Christians will read these proposals and agree with them, but still find that the victory against sin is more theoretical than actual… In their daily skirmishes against sins of lust, greed, anger, or an addiction, the sin appears to win out every time. For all their faith in God, and belief in the power of the Spirit, they feel utterly powerless.

The reality is that people in this type of situation will never begin to see victories against sin as long as their focus is on the sin itself. They need to be gripped by a vision that is bigger and more wonderful than the temporary and limited high offered by the sin. A girl who sat at night trying to remove the darkness from her room would be doomed to failure and frustration. Darkness is only driven out when the sun rises and fills that room with light. Hope comes from opening the curtains as dawn breaks. Believers struggling with a besetting sin won't get far if they worry away at the sin itself. Hope will only come as something bigger and better floods into their soul. The heart of this 'something' lies in a real and intimate encounter with God in our daily lives. But it also needs to include a vision of ourselves as we could be in the future…

Most of us overvalue the instant and undervalue the gradual. This applies particularly in our spiritual and moral lives. That is why so many of us go around looking for the 'big experience' that will for ever zap our doubts and wayward thoughts… This expectation is encouraged by the fact that the sudden and dramatic makes for livelier newspaper articles and Christian paperbacks. We are led to expect the 'quick fix' as the normal Christian life. Sometimes such instant solutions are forthcoming, but for most of us these are the exception. The real work of discipleship takes a lifetime.

An American family, the Romeros, bought Sally, a Burmese python, as a family pet when she was just one foot long. Each day they fed Sally and looked after her as a loved family member. Eight years later, Sally had grown to eleven-and-a-half feet, and weighed 80 pounds. On 20 July 1993, Sally turned on the Romeros' son, fifteen-year-old Derek, and suffocated him…

Each time we feed a sin, we are throwing another little snack to a growing snake. And a deadly snake that is full-grown will eventually turn and destroy the one who has been feeding it. The destruction wreaked by sin includes the erosion of our zest and appetite for life, a moral paralysis in which we feel unable to choose to do right any longer, the death of relationships and trust, a growing indifference towards God, even physical death itself (through drugs, suicide, murder, and so on)…

Does this mean, then, that if a Christian believer finds himself unable to stop feeding the sin snake, the snake wins in the end? That the wiles of the snake are greater than God's grace? Not a bit of it. Though we often fail, God does not easily let us go… No snake has the power to keep God's children outside his house for ever. Look again at the Bible: God's Kingdom is built with murderers, adulterers, swindlers, prostitutes and the weak in faith.

No, the snake will never have the last word. But a lifetime of daily feeding the sin snake will have two consequences for me. The first affects my lifestyle. I miss out on the fullness of life God intends for me. I accept second best, contenting myself with tacky substitutes for real love, joy and peace, when the real thing is on offer. And not only is sin second best, sin damages me. As we have noted, sin kills off whole areas of our lives, including our relationships, our sense of wonder and our capacity for making right judgments. Many people will finally stand before God, at the end of their lives, covered with the scars and bruises inflicted by the sin snake, its venom still in their veins. My sin cannot finally separate me from the love of God, but it can wreck my life.

The second consequence of feeding the sin snake is what it does to my love for God. The act of feeding that snake can have a profound effect on me, changing me into somebody who is no longer so interested in being a part of God's family. After a while, I stop even wanting God's love and forgiveness, especially if returning involves repenting. Here is the ultimate danger of daily feeding the sin snake: it hardens me into the sort of person who says 'No' to God. Feeding snakes is a deadly activity.

Feeding our children

But there are other individuals in our homes who can also be given food daily, such as our growing children. The day arrives when grown-up children leave home. We wonder how they changed from being that small, helpless baby to a healthy, intelligent, independent individual ready to make their own way in the world. The answer is that the change didn't happen suddenly or dramatically. It happened slowly, one day at a time, one meal at a time. The same is true of our spiritual and moral growth. It happens one decision at a time. Many times each day we choose what, or whom, we feed. Will we feed sins such as envy, greed, or lust? Or will we feed virtues such as self-sacrifice, faithfulness, and compassion? What we feed each day will either grow up and make us proud, or it will turn and suffocate us.

Our focus needs to be not so much on our sins, but on a vision of ourselves as we could be one day: a man or woman shaped by a lifetime of right or wrong choices, after a lifetime of feeding snakes or feeding our children. And, ultimately, our focus needs to be not on our sins, but on the One who has conquered sin: the passionate and compassionate Father who, in Christ, draws us into his family and sends his Spirit to be our strengthener and guide.

To order a copy of this book, please turn to the order form on page 159.

A decade in Oxford with BRF

Richard Fisher

Looking back at the last ten years since BRF relocated from London to Oxford, it's remarkable just how much has happened and how much we have to be thankful for.

When we moved to Oxford in August 1991, BRF had a staff of two—myself and Shelagh Brown. Shelagh had been editor of *New Daylight* since its launch in 1988, and now began to commission some adult books for us. On moving to offices owned by Lion Publishing, our staff numbers were doubled with an administrator and a secretary seconded to us from Lion. Karen Laister was that administrator in 1991—today she is our Marketing Manager!

We now have a staff of thirteen, and have just moved to new offices in north Oxford to accommodate our expanding operations. We have a full book publishing programme alongside our regular series of Bible reading notes, and a busy programme of events around which our ministry activities are based.

So what have been the significant milestones along the way?

Publishing

Shelagh did an enormous amount to put BRF 'on the map' as a book publisher, bringing some of the best-known Christian writers and communicators of the Bible to BRF. In 1994 we appointed Sue Doggett to strengthen the editorial team. Sue came to BRF with extensive experience of working with children, so in 1995 the *Barnabas* imprint was launched to provide books and resources for children under 11. In a few short years it has become recognized as a consistent source of quality Bible-related material for all who work and live with children in this age range.

In 1997 Naomi Starkey joined the team as a further commissioning editor for the adult list. Tragically, three weeks later, Shelagh died after an accident at home. Stunned by this event, we were also astounded at the sense of God's provision for BRF in bringing Naomi to the staff at just the right time.

Naomi has continued to enhance BRF's reputation for quality publishing. She has brought an even wider range of authors to BRF, consolidating our output of new books in the areas of Bible Reading and Prayer & Spirituality, while continuing to build our position as *the* UK publisher of Lent and Advent books.

Launched in 1996, the *People's Bible Commentary* is one of the key strands in BRF's publishing programme. With 18 of the 31 volumes in print, we are on course to complete the series by 2005. The series is central to BRF's objectives—addressing both head and heart, enabling people to explore the whole Bible deeply and systematically, with the help of expert commentators.

In January 1998, *Day by Day with God* was launched—the first regular Bible reading notes written by women for women. We are grateful to Mary Reid, who has done so much as editor to develop the notes.

Ministry

We feel it is not enough just to produce great books and resources—we also need to be at work among churches and congregations, helping them with Bible reading and spiritual growth, and making them aware of what we have to offer. Our heart at BRF is for *people*, and helping to resource their spiritual journey.

In 1999, all this became possible. Since then Sue Doggett has divided her time equally between working on *Barnabas* publications and establishing *Barnabas* ministry. And in July that year, Anne Hibbert joined BRF as Mission and Spirituality Adviser to develop our ministry among adults. Both Sue and Anne run annual programmes of events, including quiet days and retreats, workshops and training days, plus many speaking engagements that take BRF's ministry into the heart of the Christian community.

Since we launched our ministry appeal in December 1999 we have been deeply touched by the response that we have received from our readers and supporters who have given so generously to help us continue this work.

BRF—the organization

When BRF first moved to Oxford, we brought with us a long history of serving the church as a Bible reading agency. And we came to realize that our *new* vision for BRF's future was in fact a rediscovery of the *original* vision that had led to the founding of the organization in 1922.

In 1997 we marked BRF's 75th anniversary with a service of thanksgiving and re-dedication in Westminster Abbey and a series of events throughout the year. This year, I hope you will have been able to join us at one of the special events that have taken place to celebrate our decade in Oxford. 2002 is our 80th anniversary! Who knows what challenges and opportunities lie ahead?

I want to put on record my heartfelt thanks to all those who over the years have given so much to BRF, making us what we are today. In particular I want to thank the team here in Oxford—those mentioned already and also Dawn, Kristina, Janet, Jennifer, Lisa, Louise, Victoria and Sue. Thanks to them, BRF is a thriving organization, with a dedicated team of enthusiasts for the cause.

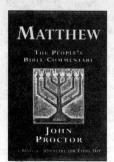

The People's Bible Commentary

The message of Matthew's Gospel is thoroughly practical, with Jesus' teaching about lifestyle and relationships having a prominent place. At the same time, it is a deeply spiritual gospel, emphasizing how the events surrounding Jesus clearly fulfilled Old Testament prophecy about the coming Messiah. The PBC *Matthew* commentary is written by the Revd John Proctor, who is based at Westminster College, Cambridge and teaches New Testament in the Cambridge Theological Federation.

MATTHEW 12:46–50

FAMILY GATHERING

We have heard nothing about Jesus' home and family life since chapter 2. He is operating away from home, moving from place to place, and using Simon Peter's house at Capernaum as an occasional base. He has gathered some followers, but has also attracted suspicion and criticism. He already seems a vulnerable, threatened and isolated figure (see 10:25; 11:19; 12:14).

He is a man apart. Yet he is not a man alone. He is shaping a community, forming a company of people where the life of God will be known in fresh ways. It takes a visit from his natural family to show, in stark and even hurtful ways, just how much he values his followers.

Mary is here, but Joseph is not mentioned; maybe he had died by this time. There were at least four brothers (Matt. 13:55–56 mentions James, Joseph, Simon and Judas) and some sisters. Indeed two of the letters in the New Testament come from two of these brothers, James and Jude. But there is no indication in Matthew's story that the brothers are men of faith at this stage.

In fact, the reverse may be true. Mark says (3:20–21) that Jesus' family were concerned about his balance of mind and had come to restrain him. That detail is missing in Matthew's version, but when we meet the family 'standing outside' we realize that they do not belong to Jesus' inner group. They address him from a distance, from the edge of the crowd, while his followers are much closer.

Family likeness

The question in verse 48 must have sounded cruel to Jesus' relatives. He sees his truest family not as the people he comes from, but as those who come with him. The family likeness is not determined by DNA and genes... The really important family likeness concerns what people do; it is a likeness of lifestyle and habit, of commitment and action.

This family likeness comes from God. Members of the family of faith show by doing God's will that they are God's children. That is the mark of true sons and daughters (cf. Matt. 21:28–31). It was the way that Jesus lived (Jn. 5:19), and is also his family's way. That does not mean, though, that Christians can ignore the needs of relatives. Jesus was very critical of people who used religion as an excuse to neglect elderly parents (15:4–6), and a similar warning comes in 1 Timothy 5:8, 16).

Jesus said, '...brother and sister and mother' (12:50). Judaism of that time usually stressed male leadership in religion, and women were often overlooked, as people whose faith need not be taken very seriously. Jesus broke with that pattern. He respected women and the faith they showed, and he wanted them among his followers, as full members of his community.

The church as family

Some Christian churches talk much about family, in an effort to strengthen and support the parents and young children in the congregation. 'Family worship' means that services are planned and led with parents and children in mind, and many other church activities have these same households in view. That pastoral concern is important, but it can sometimes be emphasized in ways that cause hurt.

Not all Christians belong to neat or easy families. Many live alone, and not all of them by choice. If family always means two parents and 2.4 children, it leaves a lot of people out. More importantly, it misses the point that the church is a new, large, inclusive, very mixed and untidy family, united in Christ, committed together to doing the will of God, and knit tight in active love. That's real good news, a pattern of community life and love to enrich and shape the whole of our living—a home that is open for all to belong and for all to enjoy.

For thought and prayer

Pause to realize—especially if following Jesus is tough at the moment — that he counts you among his family. What can you do to treat other Christians as brothers and sisters?

To order a copy of this book, please turn to the order form on page 159. Other Bible study aids published by BRF include The Ministry of the Word and the Toby and Trish series.

Christina Baxter

Suitably for a BRF Vice-President, Canon Dr Christina Baxter's call to her life's work came directly through the pages of the Bible. At the age of 15, she was reading the book of Joshua (in the Authorized Version) when the words of chapter 1 verse 8 jumped out at her: 'This book of the law shall not depart out of thy mouth; but thou shalt meditate therein day and night, that thou mayest observe to do according to all that is written therein: for then thou shalt make thy way prosperous, and then thou shalt have good success.'

For her it was a calling to study theology, rather than the science subjects that she had been expected to pursue. It led her to a university degree, followed by a stint of teaching theology in schools, and in 1979 brought her to St John's College, Nottingham, as tutor in Systematic Theology ('Christian doctrine' for the uninitiated).

Since 1997 she has been Principal of the college, immersed in balancing the needs and constraints on training people for ordained ministry in the Church of England, as well as other forms of full- and part-time Christian ministry. She says that one of the main issues that demands attention is, not surprisingly, that of finance: 'We have to train people on a shoestring—and while that's always been the case, the situation has got worse.'

The financial limitations on training budgets reflect the tension between the current situation and the hopes for the future of the Anglican Church (and indeed all Christian denominations) in this country. Although so many congregations are dwindling, active and visionary church leadership is needed not only to revitalize the faith of existing believers but to bring the gospel message a fresh audience.

'The number of folk in church is in decline and there is a major question as to what we train people for,' Christina says. 'Are we training them to manage decline or to spearhead mission? Do we focus on the Church as it is or the work of the Kingdom as it might be?'

This question of the aim of ministerial training remains a point of debate even for those in Anglican leadership. Christina has seen this unresolved debate at times leading to a conflict of assumptions between those sending people for training and those drawing up the criteria for such training. Should ordinands be learning how to manage the Church of England as it is or should they focus on mission, bringing in new members from outside?

Whatever the overall aim, the working patterns of ministry are very different from those of around 35 years ago. These days, Christina says, training colleges have to help people acquire a broader range of skills so that they can operate appropriate, flexible relationships with congregation members. Rather than running individual parishes single-handedly, clergy need to develop good teaching skills, the ability to manage teams of lay people, and the confidence to exercise oversight of others' ministries.

St John's College itself is very definitely focused on the future, reflected in a number of recent initiatives. These include the Midlands Centre for Youth Ministry which is based at the college, training youth workers on the job by day-release. *'The course combines secular youth qualification with theological input,'* says Christina. *'It's a very full and exciting programme and it's good to have clergy training alongside youth workers.'*

The college offers a new, sandwich-course method of ministerial training, so that somebody can combine being a lay worker in a parish with preparing for ordained ministry, a method which Christina feels has much to commend it.

And in terms of research, the Revd Dr Mike Moynagh is based at St John's, working on the *Tomorrow Project*. This has been set up to look at future trends in both society and church, providing the chance to do some hard thinking about possible patterns of church life in the future.

Christina has since 1985 been a member of General Synod, the Church of England's governing body. Synod is divided into the House of Bishops, the House of Clergy, and the House of Laity, and Christina chairs the House of Laity. This role means that she is also a member of the Archbishops' Council, set up to 'co-ordinate, promote, aid and further the work and mission of the Church of England' [according to the official blurb], presided over by the Archbishops of Canterbury and York.

Christina is a Church of England Reader, but has never felt called to seek ordination. Some people assume that she is ordained, as she has the title of 'Canon'. In fact it is possible to be appointed as an honorary lay canon and she is both a Canon of Southwell Minster and Canon Theologian of Coventry Cathedral.

And why did she agree to be a Vice President of BRF? *'I am in favour of reading the Bible and nobody had asked me to do anything to promote Bible reading before!'* Although her life's work has been studying theology, she firmly believes that in-depth study and devotional reading of the Bible are inextricably linked. One cannot effectively function without the other.

Guidelines © BRF 2001

The Bible Reading Fellowship
First Floor, Elsfield Hall, 15–17 Elsfield Way, Oxford OX2 8FG
ISBN 1 84101 159 2

Distributed in Australia by:
Willow Connection, PO Box 288, Brookvale, NSW 2100.
Tel: 02 9948 3957; Fax: 02 9948 8153;
E-mail: info@willowconnection.com.au
Available also from all good Christian bookshops in Australia.
For individual and group subscriptions in Australia:
Mrs Rosemary Morrall, PO Box W35, Wanniassa, ACT 2903.

Distributed in New Zealand by:
Scripture Union Wholesale, PO Box 760, Wellington
Tel: 04 385 0421; Fax: 04 384 3990; E-mail: suwholesale@clear.net.nz

Distributed in South Africa by:
Struik Book Distributors, PO Box 193, Maitland 7405, Cape Town
Tel: 021 551 5900; Fax: 021 551 1124; E-mail: enquiries@struik.co.za

Publications distributed to more than 60 countries

Printed in Denmark

BRF MINISTRY APPEAL RESPONSE FORM

Name _____

Address _____

_____ Postcode _____

Telephone _____ Email _____

(tick as appropriate)

Gift Aid Declaration

❏ I am a UK taxpayer. I want BRF to treat as Gift Aid Donations all donations I make from the date of this declaration until I notify you otherwise.

Signature _____ Date _____

❏ I would like to support BRF's ministry with a regular donation by standing order (please complete the Banker's Order below).

Standing Order – Banker's Order

To the Manager, Name of Bank/Building Society _____

Address _____

_____ Postcode _____

Sort Code _____ Account Name _____

Account No _____

Please pay Royal Bank of Scotland plc, London Drummonds Branch, 49 Charing Cross, London SW1A 2DX (Sort Code 16-00-38), for the account of BRF A/C No. 00774151

The sum of _____ pounds on ___ /___ /___ (insert date your standing order starts) and thereafter the same amount on the same day of each month until further notice.

Signature _____ Date _____

Single donation

❏ I enclose my cheque/credit card/Switch card details for a donation of
£5 £10 £25 £50 £100 £250 (other) £_____ to support BRF's ministry

Credit/ Switch card no. ▢▢▢▢▢▢▢▢▢▢▢▢▢▢▢▢▢▢▢▢

Expires ▢▢ ▢▢   Issue no. of Switch card ▢▢▢

Signature _____ Date _____

(Where appropriate, on receipt of your donation, we will send you a Gift Aid form)

❏ Please send me information about making a bequest to BRF in my will.

Please detach and send this completed form to: Richard Fisher, BRF, First Floor, Elsfield Hall, 15–17 Elsfield Way, Oxford OX2 8FG. BRF is a Registered Charity (No.233280)

BIBLE READING RESOURCES PACK

A pack of resources and ideas to help to promote Bible reading in your church is available from BRF. The pack, which will be of use at any time during the year, includes sample editions of the notes, magazine articles, leaflets about BRF Bible reading resources and much more. Unless you specify the month in which you would like the pack sent, we will send it immediately on receipt of your order. We greatly appreciate your donations towards the cost of producing the pack (without them we would not be able to make the pack available) and we welcome your comments about the contents of the pack and your ideas for future ones.

This coupon should be sent to:

BRF
First Floor
Elsfield Hall
15–17 Elsfield Way
Oxford
OX2 8FG

Name _____

Address _____

_____

_____ Postcode _____

Telephone _____

Email _____

Please send me _____ Bible Reading Resources Pack(s)

Please send the pack now/ in _____ (month).

I enclose a donation for £ _____ towards the cost of the pack.

GL0301   BRF is a Registered Charity

GUIDELINES SUBSCRIPTIONS

❑ I would like to give a gift subscription (please complete both name and address sections below)

❑ I would like to take out a subscription myself (complete name and address details only once)

This completed coupon should be sent with appropriate payment to BRF. Alternatively, please write to us quoting your name, address, the subscription you would like for either yourself or a friend (with their name and address), the start date and credit card number, expiry date and signature if paying by credit card.

Gift subscription name _____

Gift subscription address _____

_____

_____Postcode _____

Please send beginning with the January/May/September 2002 issue:
(delete as applicable)

(please tick box)	UK	SURFACE	AIR MAIL
GUIDELINES	❑ £10.50	❑ £11.85	❑ £14.10
GUIDELINES 3-year sub	❑ £26.50		

Please complete the payment details below and send your coupon, with appropriate payment to: **BRF, First Floor, Elsfield Hall, 15–17 Elsfield Way, Oxford OX2 8FG.**

Your name _____

Your address _____

_____

_____Postcode _____

Total enclosed £ _____ (cheques should be made payable to 'BRF')

Payment by cheque ❑ postal order ❑ Visa ❑ Mastercard ❑ Switch ❑

Card number: ▢▢▢▢▢▢▢▢▢▢▢▢▢▢▢▢▢▢▢▢▢

Expiry date of card: ▢▢▢▢   Issue number (Switch): ▢▢▢

Signature (essential if paying by credit/Switch card)_____

NB: BRF notes are also available from your local Christian bookshop.

GL0301   BRF is a Registered Charity

This page is intentionally left blank.

BRF PUBLICATIONS ORDER FORM

Please ensure that you complete and send off both sides of this order form.

Please send me the following book(s):

		Quantity	Price	Total
126 6	Living the Gospel (*Helen Julian CSF*)	_____	£5.99	_____
152 5	What's Wrong (*M. Starkey*)	_____	£6.99	_____
117 7	The Ministry of the Word (*Ed. N. Starkey*)	_____	£20.00	_____

Recommended for Christmas reading

136 3	The Heart of Christmas (*C. Leonard*)		£5.99	_____

Barnabas

017 0	Easy Ways to Christmas Plays (*V. Howie*)	_____	£8.99	_____
120 2	Easy Ways to Seasonal Plays (*V. Howie*)	_____	£8.99	_____
225 4	Practical Ways to Christmas Plays (*S. Jeffs*)	_____	£9.99	_____

People's Bible Commentary

030 8	PBC: 1 & 2 Samuel (*H. Mowvley*)	_____	£7.99	_____
118 5	PBC: 1 & 2 Kings (*S. Dawes*)	_____	£7.99	_____
070 7	PBC: Chronicles—Nehemiah (*M. Tunnicliffe*)	_____	£7.99	_____
031 6	PBC: Psalms 1—72 (*D. Coggan*)	_____	£7.99	_____
065 0	PBC: Psalms 73—150 (*D. Coggan*)	_____	£7.99	_____
071 5	PBC: Proverbs (*E. Mellor*)	_____	£7.99	_____
028 6	PBC: Nahum—Malachi (*G. Emmerson*)	_____	£7.99	_____
191 6	PBC: Matthew (*J. Proctor*)	_____	£7.99	_____
046 4	PBC: Mark (*D. France*)	_____	£7.99	_____
027 8	PBC: Luke (*H. Wansbrough*)	_____	£7.99	_____
029 4	PBC: John (*R.A. Burridge*)	_____	£7.99	_____
082 0	PBC: Romans (*J. Dunn*)	_____	£7.99	_____
122 3	PBC: 1 Corinthians (*J. Murphy-O'Connor*)	_____	£7.99	_____
073 1	PBC: 2 Corinthians (*A. Besançon Spencer*)	_____	£7.99	_____
012 X	PBC: Galatians and 1 & 2 Thessalonians (*J. Fenton*)	_____	£7.99	_____
119 3	PBC: Timothy, Titus and Hebrews (*D. France*)	_____	£7.99	_____
092 8	PBC: James—Jude (*F. Moloney*)	_____	£7.99	_____
3297 5	PBC: Revelation (*M. Maxwell*)	_____	£7.99	_____

Total cost of books £ _____

Postage and packing (see over) £ _____

TOTAL £ _____

See over for payment details. All prices are correct at time of going to press, are subject to the prevailing rate of VAT and may be subject to change without prior warning.

GL0301   BRF is a Registered Charity

PAYMENT DETAILS

Please complete the payment details below and send with appropriate payment and completed order form to:

**BRF, First Floor, Elsfield Hall,
15–17 Elsfield Way, Oxford OX2 8FG**

Name _____

Address _____

_____

_____ Postcode _____

Telephone _____

Email _____

Total enclosed £ _____ (cheques should be made payable to 'BRF')

Payment by cheque ❏ postal order ❏ Visa ❏ Mastercard ❏ Switch ❏

Card number: ⬜⬜⬜⬜⬜⬜⬜⬜⬜⬜⬜⬜⬜⬜⬜⬜

Expiry date of card: ⬜⬜⬜⬜   Issue number (Switch): ⬜⬜⬜⬜

Signature (essential if paying by credit/Switch card) _____

ALTERNATIVE WAYS TO ORDER

Christian bookshops: All good Christian bookshops stock BRF publications. For your nearest stockist, please contact BRF.

POSTAGE AND PACKING CHARGES				
order value	UK	Europe	Surface	Air Mail
£7.00 & under	£1.25	£2.75	£3.50	£5.50
£7.01–£30.00	£2.25	£5.50	£7.50	£11.50
Over £30.00	free	prices on request		

Telephone: The BRF office is open between 09.15 and 17.00. To place your order, ring 01865 319700.

Fax: Ring 01865 319701.

Web: Visit www.brf.org.uk

BRF is a Registered Charity